CAMBRIDGE
Global English

for Cambridge Secondary 1
English as a Second Language

Coursebook

9

Chris Barker and Libby Mitchell

CAMBRIDGE
UNIVERSITY PRESS

CAMBRIDGE
UNIVERSITY PRESS

University Printing House, Cambridge CB2 8BS, United Kingdom

Cambridge University Press is part of the University of Cambridge.

It furthers the University's mission by disseminating knowledge in the pursuit of education, learning and research at the highest international levels of excellence.

Information on this title: education.cambridge.org

© Cambridge University Press 2016

First published 2016

Printed in the United Kingdom by Latimer Trend

A catalogue record for this publication is available from the British Library

All questions, answers and annotations have been written by the authors. In examinations, the way marks are awarded may be different.

ISBN 978-1-107-68973-2 Paperback

Welcome to Cambridge Global English for Cambridge Secondary 1 English as a Second Language Stage 9

Cambridge Global English is a nine-stage course for learners of English as a Second Language (ESL). The nine stages range from the beginning of primary (Stages 1–6) to the end of junior secondary (Stages 7–9). It is ideal for all international ESL learners, and particularly for those following the Cambridge Primary/Secondary 1 curriculum framework, as it has been written to support this framework. It presents realistic listening, speaking, reading and writing tasks, as well as end-of-unit projects similar to those students might encounter in the context of a first-language school. The course is organised into 18 thematic units of study based on the Cambridge English ESL Scheme of work for Stage 9. After every other unit, there is a literature spread, featuring authentic prose, poetry and plays from a variety of sources.

Cambridge Global English materials are aligned with the Common European Framework of Reference. The materials reflect the following principles:

- *An international focus.* Specifically developed for young learners throughout the world, the topics and situations in *Cambridge Global English* have been selected to reflect this diversity and encourage learning about each other's lives through the medium of English.

- *A cross-curricular, language-rich approach to learning. Cambridge Global English* engages learners actively and creatively. At the same time as participating in a range of curriculum-based activities, they practise English language and literacy and develop critical thinking skills.

- *English for educational success.* To meet the challenges of the future, learners will need to develop skills in both conversational and more formal English. From the earliest stage, *Cambridge Global English* addresses both these competencies. Emphasis is placed on developing the listening, speaking, reading and writing skills learners will need to be successful in using English-language classroom materials.

In addition to this Coursebook, *Cambridge Global English Workbook 9* provides supplementary support and practice. Comprehensive support for teachers is available in *Cambridge Global English Teacher's Resource 9*.

We hope that learners and teachers enjoy using *Cambridge Global English Stage 9* as much as we have enjoyed writing it.

Chris Barker and Libby Mitchell

Contents

	Reading/Topic	Listening/Speaking	Use of English	Vocabulary	Writing
Unit 5 **Health and diseases**	Health, diet and exercise Illness and disease Discoveries in medicine	**Listening** Listen to a presentation about Edward Jenner **Speaking** Ask and answer questions about a sportsperson Discuss questions about diet and fitness Tell your partner information from an article	Prepositional and phrasal verbs Comparative adjectives and adverbs Prepositional and adverbial time phrases	Diet (*crave, suppress, etc.*) Medical terms (*diabetes, cells, viruses, etc.*)	A summary of a story
Project	Write a profile of a medical pioneer				
Unit 6 **Leisure time**	Leisure interests, use of digital communication and media Social media Sleep and health	**Listening** Listen to a talk about a challenge **Speaking** Ask about leisure activities Talk about not being able to use your mobile or social media	Pronouns expressing quantity in short answers (*none, hardly any, etc.*) Verbs followed by the *-ing* form Position of adverbs *just, so, really*	Discussing health issues (*at risk, exhausted, promote, etc.*)	Lists about free time Write a comment for a website
Project **Poetry** **Review**	Design and write a poster Haiku by various poets Review of Units 5–6				
Unit 7 **Energy resources**	Renewable and non-renewable sources of energy Energy efficiency	**Listening** Listen to a radio programme about energy resources in Costa Rica **Speaking** Discuss advantages and disadvantages of types of energy generation	Determiners and pre-determiners (*some of the beaches*) Compound adjectives Future continuous	Environment (*eco-friendly, low-energy, energy-efficient, etc.*)	Profile of a country: Sweden Energy-efficient features for your school
Project	Write a short report about energy generation				
Unit 8 **Industrial revolution**	The importance of water in farming The start of the Industrial Revolution in Britain Developments in food technology	**Listening** Listen to a programme about the Industrial Revolution **Speaking** Discuss agriculture in your country Talk about being a child during the Industrial Revolution in Britain Discuss ways of preserving food	The passive (*It is thought that, It is thought to be*) Past perfect continuous Relative pronouns	The Industrial Revolution (*farm, mill, factory, steam engine, etc.*)	A paragraph about agriculture in your region for a web-based guide An account of a day in the life of a factory worker in the 18th century
Project **Memoir** **Review**	Industry in my country *A Yorkshire Childhood* by George Oldfield Review of Units 7–8				
Unit 9 **Handling data**	Statistics Reporting facts Collecting data	**Listening** Listen to students talking about the results of a test **Speaking** Discuss and compare the results of a test Discuss data in articles Discuss the banning of mobile phones in schools Discuss the cost of a watch using *median* and *mean*	Comparatives and superlatives (*more, most, less, least, fewer, the fewest*) Complex noun phrases	The language of statistics (*mode, median, mean, range*)	An article for a newspaper about banning mobile phones in school
Project	Design and write a questionnaire				

	Reading/Topic	Listening/Speaking	Use of English	Vocabulary	Writing
Unit 10 **Giving presentations**	Giving presentations and speeches Presentation software	**Listening** Listen to a speech **Speaking** Discuss advice Comment on presentation slides Discuss a speech A profile of an English-speaking country	Prepositional and phrasal verbs Reported speech – statements Pre-verbal adverbs (*first of all, next, finally*)	Language for presentations (*I'm going to talk about…, The next issue…, To sum up, etc.*)	An end-of-term speech A proposal for an English evening
Project **Non-fiction** **Review**	Prepare and give a presentation *A Little History of the World* by E.H. Gombrich Review of Units 9–10				
Unit 11 **Learning and training**	Teaching and learning Practical skills training School life	**Listening** Listen to short presentations from a careers day at a school **Speaking** Discuss what kind of skills and knowledge a person needs for certain jobs Answer questions about practical training tasks	Prepositional and phrasal verbs to do with learning Quantifiers with uncountable nouns (*a piece of advice*) Present perfect simple and present perfect continuous	Collocations (*overcome a fear, dress wounds, build team spirit*) Idioms (*loads of, to get the hang of, the best ever, etc.*)	A profile of yourself as a learner
Project	Write a page for the school website				
Unit 12 **Making a living**	Jobs and aspects of work Part-time and summer jobs Young entrepreneurs	**Listening** Listen to teenagers discussing jobs **Speaking** Discuss jobs and their advantages Discuss part-time jobs in your country Ask and answer about part-time jobs Discuss entrepreneurial competitions	Relative clauses with *which* referring to a whole clause Reflexive pronoun structures Present continuous passive	Jobs (*doctor, chef, graphic designer, vet, manager, etc.*)	A paragraph explaining your first choice of job A report about whether part-time jobs are a good idea
Project **Fiction** **Review**	An application for a competition *The Adventures of Tom Sawyer* by Mark Twain Review of Units 11–12				
Unit 13 **Population and resources**	Population distribution and density Population pyramids Population and migration Vital resources – water	**Listening** Listen to a radio report **Speaking** Discuss why geographical features affect where people live Discuss possible reasons for changes in the shape of population pyramids	Prepositions in the context of numbers and data The future perfect Conjunctions	Discussing resources (*essential, finite, consumers, etc.*)	Write questions about resources
Project	Water for the future				
Unit 14 **Cultures and customs**	Naming customs Ceremonies and special occasions Proverbs	**Listening** Listen to people talking about their names Listen for inconsistencies **Speaking** Discuss naming traditions and names in your country Discuss your name Discuss the meaning of proverbs	Participle clauses Present simple passive	Collocations associated with engagement and marriage (*to mark an engagement, to set a date, to exchange rings, etc.*) Proverbs	A paragraph about names in your country A paragraph describing engagement and or marriage traditions in your country Write about proverbs
Project **Fiction** **Review**	Write a short story *They Don't Mean It!* By Lensey Namioka Review of Units 13–14				

	Reading/Topic	Listening/Speaking	Use of English	Vocabulary	Writing
Unit 15 **The digital age**	Using print and digital resources Developments in technology The advantages and disadvantages of digital technology	**Listening** Listen to telephone conversations about IT problems Listen to an interview about using digital devices **Speaking** Discuss the advantages and disadvantages of handwriting Discuss the advantages and disadvantages of robots Give your opinions on using digital devices	Prepositional and phrasal verbs to do with using technology (*log in, click on, etc.*) Focusing adverbs (*only, just, simply, etc.*) Adverbs of degree (*extremely, quite, etc.*)	Print and digital resources (*diary, calendar, etc.*) Technology (*display, aerodynamics, adapt, etc*)	Instructions to explain how to do something on your computer
Project	Write a report for a technology magazine				
Unit 16 **Light and sound**	Optical illusions The perception of colour Sounds in language	**Listening** Listen to a news report on colour perception Listen to onomatopoeic words **Speaking** Discuss Pepper's ghost Discuss optical illusions Invent a story using onomatopoeic words	Prepositional phrases Conjunctions followed by *-ing* forms	Visual perception (*wavelength, retina, colour-blind, etc.*) Onomatopoeic words (*roar, rumble, banging, buzzing, etc.*)	A description of a play for a diary entry
Project **Poetry** **Review**	Write a story using onomatopoeic words *The Sound Collector* by Roger McGough; *SSHH!* by Les Baynton Review of Units 15–16				
Unit 17 **Right and wrong**	Crime Moral responsibility and citizenship	**Listening** Listen to people describing crimes **Speaking** Discuss the minimal age of criminal responsibility Discuss crimes and appropriate punishments Discuss what you would have done in certain situations	Prepositional verbs to do with crime The third conditional	Crime (*thief, steal, arsonist, etc.*)	A statement describing what happened in a crime
Project	Write a witness statement				
Unit 18 **A performance in English**	Theatre traditions People who work in the theatre Scriptwriting	**Listening** Listen to someone talk about roles in the theatre **Speaking** Discuss things you enjoyed doing as a child	*Used to* and *would* for repeated actions and events in the past Prepositions following nouns and adjectives	Theatre (*actor, playwright, producer, director, etc.*)	Things you enjoyed doing as a child Descriptions of people you know The advantages and disadvantages of being a professional actor
Project **Fiction** **Review**	Write a script for a scene from *Diary of an (Un)teenager* – the play *The No. 1 Ladies' Detective Agency* by Alexander McCall Smith Review of Units 17–18				

1 Family ties

- **Topics** Family members; twins; family life
- **Use of English** Pronouns and determiners:
  both (of), each other / one another, either of / neither of; reporting verbs (*offer, suggest*, etc.)

Family life

- Why are families important?

Reading

1 Read the magazine article. How many people live together in each family?

Dan lives in Liverpool with his mum, dad and ten brothers and sisters. The two oldest children in the family, David and Sara, are in fact Dan's stepbrother and stepsister.

'Because there are so many of us, we all have to help with jobs around the house. It's OK, though. We sometimes argue and the house can be really noisy at times but we have a lot of fun and we get on well most of the time. And of course, we've got a ready-made football team! The only problem is that the queue for the bathroom in the morning is quite long!'

Hua lives in Shenyang. She's an only child.

'I have no siblings and both my parents are only children so I have no cousins, aunts or uncles. But I've never felt lonely because I've always had lots of friends. My grandparents looked after me when I was little, so I'm very close to them, especially my maternal grandmother. I still visit all my grandparents in the holidays.'

Yousef lives in Tunis with his parents and his three brothers.

'I don't have much time for my own interests. There's a lot of pressure to do well at school, which means I get a lot of homework, and I often have to stay in to look after my brothers when my parents are at work because I'm the oldest. I think my youngest brother is spoilt. He never gets told off – he gets away with everything.'

Salma lives in Dubai with her parents, her brother and her sister-in-law.

'My brother is ten years older than me. He's married and my sister-in-law has just had a baby. My friends think it's really funny that I'm 14 and I'm already an aunt! But I love it. My nephew is just six weeks old. He's so cute.'

2 Which of the following are implied in the text?

1 Dan doesn't mind doing jobs at home.
2 Dan's parents are very strict.
3 Hua is sad that she hasn't got any brothers and sisters.
4 Hua gets on well with her grandparents.
5 Yousef isn't entirely happy with his life.
6 Yousef feels his parents aren't always fair in the way they treat the children.
7 Salma gets on well with her parents.
8 Salma is annoyed at her friends' reaction to her being an aunt.

Vocabulary

3 Find the words in the text for the following.

1 the son of your stepmother or stepfather
2 the daughter of your stepmother or stepfather
3 someone without brothers or sisters
4 brothers and sisters
5 your aunt and uncle's children
6 your mother's mother
7 your brother's wife
8 your brother's or sister's son

4 Match the following words to the definitions.

1 your father's mother   ● maternal grandfather
2 your mother's father   ● niece
3 your sister's husband   ● paternal grandmother
4 your brother's or   ● brother-in-law
  sister's daughter

Language tip

Formal	Informal
mother	mum
father	dad
grandmother	grandma, granny
grandfather	grandad, grandpa

Speaking

5 Work in small groups. Tell each other about your family. Ask and answer these questions.

1 Have you got brothers and sisters?

2 Do you spend time with your grandparents?

3 Do you get on well with all the members of your family?

4 What responsibilities do you have at home?

5 Are there any things at home that you would change?

Writing

6 Write a paragraph about your family for the magazine article in Exercise 1.

Try to use the following phrasal verbs.

get on well with
look after
get told off (for doing something)
get away with

Twins reunited

- What are the advantages and disadvantages of being a twin?

Reading

1 This story appeared in an online newspaper. Why do you think it made the news?

Identical twin sisters, separated at birth and brought up 4000 miles apart, describe the moment they discovered each other on Facebook

Anaïs Bordier was brought up as an only child in Paris, while Samantha Futerman grew up as the only adopted child in a New Jersey family.

But while Anaïs was studying fashion design in London, she was shown a YouTube video of an American actress who looked, sounded and acted just like her. So she sent a Facebook message to Samantha, who was born on the same day in Busan, South Korea. Then they talked on Skype for three hours. One year and one DNA test later, they knew that they were twin sisters that had been separated at birth. Both Anaïs and Samantha speak English, although French is Anaïs's first language.

The girls say they both felt that something was missing in their lives but now that they have found each other, they have extra confidence.

Anaïs said, 'I did feel as if I missed something. I had an imaginary friend when I was a kid and she was called Anne. I needed that comfort, I guess.'

Neither the Futermans nor the Bordier family knew that the baby they had adopted was a twin. Mrs Futerman said, 'We would have taken both of you'.

Anaïs and Samantha met for the first time in London and realised just how much they have in common. They look alike, they have similar mannerisms and they share the same interests. Both of them are interested in the arts, they have the same favourite TV programmes, they both hate cooked carrots and neither of them likes getting up early.

Has either of them ever pretended to be the other one? They're not saying ...

2 This story originally appeared with three bullet points below the headline. The bullet points summarised the story. This is a feature of some online news reporting. Read the story and complete the three points.

1. ● Anaïs Bordier and Samantha Futerman were born ... and adopted by ...
2. ● Anaïs grew up in ... and Samantha grew up in ...
3. ● They got in touch with one another after ...

Did you know?

There are two types of twins: identical and fraternal (non-identical). Identical twins have very similar DNA, whereas fraternal twins each have their own, different, DNA. In fact identical twins aren't completely identical, although they look very similar. For example, their fingerprints are similar but not identical. Fraternal twins, on the other hand, can look quite different from each other.

Look carefully at the photo of Samantha and Anaïs. Can you see any differences?

3 Discuss the following question:

Why do online journalists summarise a news story in bullet points to introduce it?

4 Complete the chart about Anaïs and Samantha.

	Anaïs	Samantha
1 place of birth	Busan, South Korea	Busan, South Korea
2 as a child, lived in		
3 job / studying		
4 first language		
5 likes		
6 dislikes		

5 Read what Leyla says. Use the words and phrases in red in the Use of English box to complete the sentences.

I live in the north of Amman. My cousin lives in the south of the city, not far from the airport. I usually phone her on Saturday, or she phones me. I'm an only child and so is she. We've got another cousin in Canada and one in France, but we've never met them.

1 We _____ live in Amman.
2 _____ us live in Amman.
3 _____ my cousin and I live in Amman.
4 We phone _____ at the weekend.
5 _____ us has brothers and sisters.
6 We've got a cousin in Canada and one in France but we've never met _____ them.

Use of English: *both (of), each other one another, either of / neither of*

both

Use *both* to talk about two people (or things) together.
Both Anaïs and Samantha speak English.
Both girls were born on the same day.

Note that *both* comes after a subject pronoun, e.g. *we, you, they*.
They both hate cooked carrots. NOT ~~Both they hate cooked carrots.~~

both of

Use *both of* before the object pronouns *us, you, them*.
Both of them are interested in the arts.

each other / one another

Each other and *one another* mean the same.
They discovered each other on Facebook.
They got in touch with one another.

either of / neither of

Use *either* when you mean 'one or the other'.
Has either of them ever pretended to be the other one?
Use *neither* when you mean 'not one and not the other'.
Neither of them likes getting up early.
We usually use *either* and *neither* with a singular verb.

both, either, neither

Don't use *both* in negative sentences.
Say: *I don't like either tea or coffee* NOT ~~I don't like both tea and coffee.~~
I don't like either of them NOT ~~I don't like both of them.~~
Neither my mum nor my dad speaks French NOT ~~Both my mum and my dad don't speak French.~~
Neither of them speaks French NOT ~~Both of them don't speak French.~~

Speaking

6 In small groups, ask and answer.

1 Who are you most like in your family?
2 What are the physical similarities between you?
3 What else do you have in common?

Well done!

● When do people congratulate others, apologise or complain? Give examples.

I'm sorry

The neighbours have been complaining about your music. Please keep the volume down or use your headphones.

Mum

Congratulations on passing your exams!

Listening 2

1 Listen to these seven conversations. Match each one to a sentence.

a She offered to carry his shopping.

b He congratulated her on doing so well in her exam.

c He reminded her to take her sports kit to school.

d He forgave him for taking his bike without telling him.

e The neighbours complained about having no electricity.

f He suggested going to a restaurant.

g She apologised for making a lot of noise.

Language tip

Learn these verbs with their dependent prepositions:

accuse (someone) of

apologise for

blame (someone) for

complain about

congratulate (someone) on

forgive (someone) for

insist on

Remember that they are all followed by a verb in the *-ing* form.

Use of English: Reporting verbs

When you report what someone said, you can use a verb such as *offer, remind, suggest, complain, apologise, congratulate, forgive*.

Verb (+ object) + *to* infinitive	Other reporting verbs which are followed by the *to* infinitive:
She offered to carry his shopping.	*agree, decide, promise, refuse*
He reminded her to take her sports kit to school.	
Verb + *-ing* form	Other reporting verbs which are followed by the *-ing* form:
He suggested going to a restaurant.	*recommend, deny*
Verb (+ object) + preposition + *-ing* form	Other reporting verbs which are followed by a preposition and the *-ing* form:
The neighbours complained about having no electricity in their flat.	*accuse, blame, insist*
We apologised for making a lot of noise.	
He congratulated her on doing so well in her exam.	
He forgave him for taking his bike without telling him.	

2 Use the verb given to report what each person said.

1 Tom: I know I didn't do well in the exam but I will try harder next time.
(use *promise*) Tom *promised to try harder next time.*

2 Mrs Bennett: Can I make you a sandwich, Alex?
(use *offer*) Mrs Bennett _____

3 Luke: Come and play football, Hugo.
Hugo: No, I'm going to finish the crossword first!
(use *insist*) Hugo _____ .

4 Soraya: You took my mobile phone.
Soraya's sister: I didn't!
(use *accuse*) Soraya _____ .

5 Mum: Don't forget to switch the lights off before you go to bed, Anita.
(use *remind*) Mum _____ .

Writing

3 Read Amir's note of apology. How does he structure it? Complete these sentences.

1 He starts by ...
2 Then he ...
3 Finally he ...

Dear Mrs Turner,

I apologise for being late for school twice this week. My parents are away at the moment and my grandparents are looking after me. They don't have a car so I have to take the bus to school. The bus has been late because there's a lot of traffic. I'm really sorry about this. I'll try my best to be on time in the future.

Yours sincerely,

Amir

4 Write a note of apology to your teacher based on the following situation.

Yesterday, you left school early without permission. You had an appointment at the dentist and you only remembered at the last minute.

Project: A scene from family life

5 Write a short script for a typical morning at home with your family.

- It can be realistic or comic.
- Include some of the reporting verbs in the Use of English box.
- Here are some examples:

It's 7.30 a.m. Sara, Nina and Mum are in the kitchen.

Sara: There's no orange juice left. You've drunk it all, Nina.

Nina: No, I haven't. Mum! Sara's just accused me of drinking all the juice.

Mum: Don't worry, girls. Just remind me to get some on the way home.

Faisal is shouting from the bathroom. Jawed is in his room getting ready for school.

Faisal: Arrgh! The shower is freezing. It's your fault, Jawed.

Jawed: Don't blame me for using all the hot water. I was only in the shower for a few minutes.

Dad is in the kitchen and Daniel, aged 6, comes in holding his elbow.

Daniel: Oh, Dad, I fell down the stairs. I've hurt my elbow.

Dad: Well, why do you insist on wearing those ridiculous slippers? You know you always fall over in them.

Personal appearance

- **Topics** Traditional clothes and clothes for special occasions; attitudes to fashion; classic items of clothing
- **Use of English** Compound adjectives; *-ing* forms used as subjects, objects and complements; forming questions

All dressed up

- Look at the people in the pictures. Which of these words would you use to describe what the people in picture 1 are wearing?

traditional	formal	informal

  Would you use the same words for the people in picture 2?

Picture 1

Picture 2

Reading

1 Read about traditional Indonesian dress and find the items in italics in picture 1.

A *saput* is a piece of cloth worn by Balinese men and boys as part of their traditional temple dress. It is worn from waist to knee over the *kamben*, a wider piece of fabric worn from waist to ankle. Men and boys wear the kamben tied in the centre, whereas women and girls tie it at the side. Men and boys also wear a headdress called an *udeng*. If the ceremony is informal, an ordinary shirt is worn, but if the ceremony is an important one, a white shirt with gold buttons is required. Women and girls wear a long-sleeved lacy blouse with loose sleeves called a *kebaya* with a kamben, although in the past, for formal ceremonies, they wore a tight-fitting piece of material round their body and over the shoulder.

2 Answer the questions.

1 Where have the teenagers in picture 1 just been?
2 Was the occasion formal or informal?

Use of English: Compound adjectives

You can use two words together, often linked with a hyphen, to make a compound adjective: for example, 'a long-sleeved blouse' (= 'a blouse with long sleeves'), 'a tight-fitting piece of material' (= a piece of material which fits tightly).

3 Write the name of an item of clothing which each of the following compound adjectives could describe.

1 short-sleeved *a short-sleeved shirt*
2 ankle-length
3 knee-length
4 high-heeled
5 highly-patterned
6 brightly-coloured

Language tip

Some compound adjectives, such as *handmade*, *homemade* and *waterproof*, used to be hyphenated (*hand-made*, *home-made*, *water-proof*) but today they're written as one word.

Writing

4 Write a description of what the people in picture 2 are wearing.

Remember to:

- describe the colour
- mention any particular features (*with a collar / a pocket / buttons down the front*)
- use compound adjectives where you can.

5 Give your description to your partner to read and check. Is there anything you want to add to your description, or change? Write a final version.

Speaking

6 Think of a formal occasion which you or a member of your family attended. Describe what you / they wore. Your partner must take notes as you are speaking. When you have finished, check your partner's notes.

My style

● How would you describe your attitude to clothes and fashion?

Reading

1 Match the texts to the pictures.

Gabriel | Mayar | Becky | Ricky

❶ 'Shopping for clothes doesn't interest me. It's so time-consuming. Anyway, I'm much more comfortable in sports clothes. I just don't feel like me if I'm all dressed up. I wear casual clothes – jeans, sports shoes, sweatshirts, stuff like that. I like bright colours. It's fashionable for girls to have their hair coloured but I don't have mine done.'

❷ 'How would I describe my attitude to clothes? Well, I wouldn't say I was fashion-conscious but I like clothes that are quite stylish and that fit well. I try to choose colours that suit me, like blue. I don't like tight-fitting clothes but I don't like baggy clothes either. I might wear tracksuit bottoms at home but I'd never go out in them.'

❸ 'People say I look scruffy but I don't care what I look like. All I need is an old T-shirt, a pair of jeans and some canvas shoes. I can't imagine anything worse than spending a Saturday afternoon shopping for clothes. And another thing I really don't like is wearing formal clothes. Don't even go there! We had a family photo taken for my sister's wedding and I had to look smart. I had to wear a shirt and a tie. I didn't recognise myself!'

❹ 'I like wearing pastel shades like pale blue and pale pink. I think they suit me. I like to look nice but I don't like to stand out from the crowd. I definitely don't follow the style of any celebrities. I look at what girls my own age are wearing.'

Language tip

Remember to use the structure *have something done* when you don't do something for yourself but someone does it for you.

It's fashionable for girls to have their hair *coloured.*

have / had	+	object	+	past participle

We had *a family photo* taken *for my sister's wedding.*

2 Work in pairs. Find these words in the text and say what they mean.

1 casual
2 fashion-conscious
3 stylish
4 baggy
5 scruffy
6 formal
7 smart
8 pastel

3 Find at least three things in the four texts that you would say about yourself. Write them down.

I wouldn't say I was fashion-conscious. ...

4 Work in pairs. What would you say about your partner's attitude towards clothes and fashion? Write three or four sentences.

He / She likes clothes that are quite stylish and fit well.

Speaking

5 Tell your partner what you've written about him / her. Does he / she agree?

I'd say that you like clothes that are quite stylish and fit well.

Yes, I'd agree with that. / No, I wouldn't agree with that. I'm not really interested in style.

Use of English: *-ing* forms used as subjects, objects and complements (after the verb *to be*)

subject

Shopping (for clothes) doesn't interest me.

object

I like wearing pastel shades.

complement (after the verb *to be*)

And another thing I really don't like is wearing formal clothes.

---

6 Complete these sentences so that they are true for you.

1 _____ing (...) doesn't interest me.
2 I like _____ing (...).
3 Something I really don't like is _____ing (...).

Listening 3

7 Listen to Ricky, from Exercise 1, talking to his friend, Sam. What is Sam surprised about?

8 Reread Ricky's text in Exercise 1 (text 3). Listen again and write down the inconsistency between what Ricky says in the text and what he says in his conversation with Sam.

Writing

9 Write a paragraph describing your own attitude to clothes and fashion, like the ones in Exercise 1.

I like wearing casual clothes. I don't like tight-fitting clothes. I'm much more comfortable in sports clothes. ...

I suppose I'm quite fashion-conscious. Looking good is important to me. At home, I might wear tracksuit bottoms and a T-shirt, but I like to look nice when I go out. ...

A fashion classic

● What makes an item of clothing a fashion classic?

Reading

1 Read the article. How did René Lacoste influence tennis fashion?

The history of the polo shirt

In the 19th and early 20th centuries, tennis was very much a sport of the upper and middle classes. Tennis players were expected to look very smart and formal. ...[1]

Then, in 1926, at the US Open Championship, the French tennis player René Lacoste wore a shirt which he himself had designed. It created a sensation. Instead of having long sleeves which the players wore rolled up, the Lacoste shirt had short sleeves and a collar which could be turned up to protect the neck from the sun. ...[2]

The same year, Lacoste's friend, Robert George, drew him a picture of a crocodile with its mouth open. This was because Lacoste was known as 'The Crocodile' by his fans, due to his tenacity on court. ...[3]

In 1933, André Gillier, the owner of a large clothing factory in France, went into business with Lacoste and began to manufacture the short-sleeved Lacoste shirt with the crocodile logo on it. The shirts soon became popular with tennis players and other sportspeople. ...[4]

Nowadays, the polo shirt is a classic item of 'smart casual' dress. It's more formal than a T-shirt but less formal than a long-sleeved shirt. ...[5]

2 Choose a sentence to complete each paragraph in the article.

a Polo players, for example, swapped their long-sleeved, heavy cotton shirts for Lacoste's short-sleeved shirts and gave the shirt its name – the polo shirt.

b It has even become a standard item of school uniform throughout the world.

c Lacoste had the crocodile embroidered onto his blazer, which he wore to matches.

d It was made of soft cotton and was comfortable, light and cool.

e Men wore long-sleeved white shirts, white trousers and ties and women wore ankle-length, long-sleeved dresses and hats.

3 Match the words to the definitions.

1	created a sensation	**a**	a design or symbol used by a company to advertise its products
2	tenacity	**b**	a smart jacket, often worn as part of school uniform or by members of a sports club
3	embroidered	**c**	accepted as normal
4	blazer	**d**	caused a lot of excitement, surprise or interest
5	manufacture	**e**	decorated by sewing small patterns or pictures in coloured thread (onto a piece of cloth)
6	logo		
7	polo	**f**	determination to do something, even if it takes a long time and is difficult
8	swapped	**g**	exchanged
9	standard	**h**	produce something, usually in large numbers in a factory
		i	a game played between two teams who ride horses and hit a ball with long wooden hammers

4 Write seven questions about the history of the polo shirt to ask your partner. Refer to the complete article (that is, include the sentences from Exercise 2). Use the following prompts.

	Partner A	Partner B
Paragraph 1	**1** Who played ...?	**1** How were ... ?
	2 What did men ...?	**2** What did women ...?
Paragraph 2	**3** What happened ...?	**3** What was ... like?
Paragraph 3	**4** Why did ... ?	**4** What did ...?
	5 Who was ...?	**5** When did ...?
Paragraph 4	**6** What logo ...?	**6** Who wore ...?
Paragraph 5	**7** Is the polo shirt more ... than ...?	**7** What has ...?

Speaking

5 Work in pairs. Take turns to ask and answer the questions you wrote for Exercise 4.

A: *Who played tennis in the 19th and early 20th centuries?*

B: *The upper and middle classes.*

Project: A classic item of clothing

6 Research another item of clothing, such as the kimono, the abaya, the baseball cap, the T-shirt or jeans. Write an article about it for a website on the history of clothing.

- Plan your article. You can divide it into the following sections: 'Introduction', 'History' and 'Today'.
- Find illustrations to accompany the article.
- Write a first draft.
- Show your draft to other students and ask them to comment on and proofread it.
- Write a final version, taking into account the comments and corrections.

Fiction

Diary of an (Un)teenager
Pete Johnson

1 Why do people keep diaries? What do they write in them?

2 Read the extract. Who is Zac? How are Zac and Spencer different?

3 Read the extract again and answer the questions.

1 Why does Zac phone Spencer?
2 Why does Spencer step back in horror when he sees Zac?
3 Why does Zac swallow hard before he tells Spencer that he is a skater now?
4 Why does Zac smile at Spencer and why can't Spencer smile back?
5 Why does Spencer ask Zac if he's still got the receipt?
6 What does Zac mean when he says 'I've got to be something'? Why does his voice rise when he says it?

4 Answer these questions about the style of the extract.

1 What is the effect of using words such as *horror, shock, huge, massive*?
2 What do you notice about the length of the sentences and of the paragraphs?
3 Why does the writer use direct speech rather than reported speech?

Language tip

Look at these three sentences. Notice how the words in red add emphasis and make the sentences sound more dramatic.

Why on earth are you dressed like that?

But you haven't even got a skateboard.

It's ever since I turned 13.

5 Work in groups. Discuss these questions.

1 Why is the title of the book *Diary of an (Un)teenager*?
2 The extract is from the first chapter of the book.
What do you think the theme of the book is going to be?

Diary of an (Un)teenager
Chapter 1
A Terrible Shock

Friday, May 29ᵗʰ

Strange things have started happening. I feel the need to write these important events down in a diary.

Zac rang me this evening, dear diary. He said, "Hi, Spencer! When you see me
5   tonight you may get a shock!"

He wouldn't say any more.

He was upstairs when I went round to his house.

I opened the door to his bedroom and then stepped back in horror.

I'd never expected this.

10   I blinked. But Zac was still there – and wearing … a blue shirt that looked
huge on him, the baggiest white trousers I'd ever seen and massive trainers with
a huge flap and no laces.

"Why on earth are you dressed like that?" I gasped.

Zac swallowed hard, then announced, "Because, Spencer, I'm a skater now."

15   "But you haven't even got a skateboard."

"Not yet, I haven't," he agreed. "But I'm getting one next week. And you don't
really need a skateboard these days. You've just got to have the right gear."

Then he put on this top with a hood.

"Once you've got your hoodie, you're a skater. It's as simple as that."

20   He smiled at me. I tried to smile back but I just couldn't.

"So how much did all this gear cost you?" I asked. "And have you still got the
receipt?"

Zac whispered the price to me. I nearly passed out with shock. He'd used up
all his birthday money on this rubbish. And nearly half of all his savings too.

25   I just couldn't believe it.

Zac and I had never wasted any of our money on clothes before. We'd been
fine wearing the same shirt and jeans for years.

So what had happened to him?

"Just why have you decided to be a skater?" I asked, finding it hard to control
30   my voice.

Zac started pacing around his room. He sighed heavily.

"It's ever since I turned 13. It's made me think about my life." His voice rose.
"I've got to be something."

…

Will I soon start throwing all my money away on stupid clothes?

35   No, dear diary, I won't.

I am going to stay EXACTLY as I am now.

And that's a promise, signed here in my diary.

by Pete Johnson

blinked (*line 10*) quickly closed and then opened [his] eyes

massive (*line 11*) very big

flap (*line 12*) a piece of material fixed along one edge, used for covering or closing something

laces (*line 12*) strings used to tie shoes

gasped (*line 13*) breathed in suddenly because [he] was shocked

swallowed (*line 14*) made a movement in [his] throat as if to make food or drink go down

gear (*line 17*) (*slang*) clothes and things you use for a particular purpose

hood (*line 18*) the part of a coat or jacket that covers your head and neck

hoodie (*line 19*) a jacket or sweatshirt with a hood

receipt (*line 22*) a piece of paper which shows you have paid for something

whispered (*line 23*) said something very quietly

passed out (*line 23*) became unconscious

used up (*line 23*) used completely so there was nothing left

savings (*line 24*) money that you have saved

sighed (*line 31*) breathed out slowly, making a noise

rose (*line 32*) (*past tense of 'rise'*) went up

Review of Units 1–2

Vocabulary

Family members

1 Which of the following are male? Which are female? Which can be either male or female? Write 'm' for male, 'f' for female and 'm / f' for male or female.

1 aunt	**7** only child
2 grandpa	**8** paternal grandmother
3 granny	
4 maternal grandfather	**9** sibling
5 nephew	**10** stepsister
6 niece	**11** twins
	12 uncle

2 What's the word for:

1 your sister's husband?
2 your stepfather's daughter?
3 your mother's mother?
4 your aunt's son?
5 siblings of the same age?

Style of clothes

3 Choose the correct word for each picture.

1

a casual
b scruffy
c baggy

2

a short-sleeved
b knee-length
c long-sleeved

3

a smart
b casual
c baggy

4

a scruffy
b casual
c formal

5

a embroidered
b pastel shades
c lacy

Use of English

4 Choose the correct option in each case.

My friend and I are quite similar. We've known *one another / both*[1] since we were 5 years old. *Both of / Either of*[2] us like sports clothes but *either of / neither of*[3] us likes shopping. It's quite funny because sometimes when we see *both of us / each other*[4] at the weekend, we're wearing identical T-shirts. One thing you can be sure of is that you'll never see *either of / both of*[5] us in a suit and tie because we don't like formal clothes.

5 Complete each sentence with the correct preposition:

of   for   about   on

1 I was so pleased when the teacher congratulated me _____ writing an excellent essay.
2 I was accused _____ being late but it wasn't my fault!
3 Forgive me _____ interrupting, but someone wants to speak to you.
4 I don't blame you _____ falling asleep during that film. It was very long.
5 The Maths teacher complained _____ the noise.

6 It's only a short distance from my friend's house, but his parents always insist _____ driving me home.

7 They apologised _____ leaving early but they had to get the last bus home.

6 Complete the sentences with the verbs in the box in the correct form: the *to* infinitive or the *-ing* form.

> help   show   go   look at   break   take   send

1 He refused _____ at the answers until he'd finished the Sudoku puzzle.

2 I promised _____ my parents a text to say I'd arrived safely.

3 He denied _____ the window but the headteacher saw him kick the ball.

4 Our friends suggested _____ a picnic to the beach.

5 Remind me _____ you my new trainers.

6 She offered _____ me with my Maths homework.

7 Would you recommend _____ to Canada for a summer holiday?

7 Rewrite the descriptions using a compound adjective.

1 a shirt with short sleeves   *a short-sleeved shirt*

2 a coat which comes down to your ankles

3 a pair of shoes with high heels

4 a dress which comes down to your knees

5 a shirt with long sleeves

6 a scarf in bright colours

8 Rewrite these sentences starting with the words given.

1 I really enjoy seeing friends at the weekend.
   Something I really enjoy is seeing friends at the weekend.

2 It's very important to me to spend time with my family.
   Spending ...

3 It's great to have lots of cousins.
   Having ...

4 I really don't like wearing bright colours.
   Something ...

5 I don't wear baggy clothes because they don't suit me.
   I don't like ...

General knowledge quiz

9 Work in pairs. Ask and answer the questions.

1 What relation to you is your brother's son?

2 What relation to your father is your maternal grandfather?

3 There is one way in which you can tell identical twins apart. What is it?

4 What are fraternal twins?

5 Is an *udeng* a headdress, a shirt for formal occasions or a piece of fabric worn from waist to ankle?

6 In which country would you be if you saw someone wearing an *udeng*?

7 What sport did René Lacoste play and what nationality was he?

8 What is the logo that appears on a Lacoste shirt and why?

9 Look at the photo. What's the sport and what is the connection with René Lacoste?

10 What do you call a jacket which is often worn as part of a school uniform or by members of a sports club?

3 Moods and feelings

- **Topics** Emotions, moods and feelings; school life (problems and solutions); non-verbal communication (gestures, eye contact, etc.)
- **Use of English** Past modal forms: *must have*, *might have*, *can't have*; present continuous with *always*; abstract nouns

Ups and downs

- Would you describe yourself as an emotional person? Why?

Vocabulary

1 How do you think these people are feeling? Write an adjective for each photo. Compare your ideas. Did you all write the same words?

2 Work with a partner. Put the words and phrases which have a similar meaning into groups. Make a separate list of those which don't fit into a group.

angry	delighted	feeling a bit down	nervous
annoyed	depressed	frightened	sad
anxious	disappointed	furious	terrified
apprehensive	ecstatic	in a bad mood	thrilled
bored	excited	miserable	upset
confused	embarrassed	mixed up	worried

3 Compare the words and phrases in your list with what other people have written. Explain and justify your choices.

Pair 1: We've put *angry, annoyed, furious* and *in a bad mood* in the same group.

Pair 2: We didn't include *in a bad mood* because that's different from being angry, annoyed or furious.

4 Are there any more words or phrases you can use now to describe the people in the photos in Exercise 1?

5 Find a photo in Exercise 1 to match each of these descriptions.

a She's absolutely furious. Something bad must have happened. She might have just finished some work on the computer and the computer's crashed so she's lost all her work.

b He looks a bit down. I think he's had some news and it can't have been good news.

Use of English: *must have, might have, can't have* + past participle

You can use:

- *must have* to talk about things you feel sure have happened.
  Something bad must have happened.

- *might have* to talk about things which have perhaps happened.
  She might have won a competition.

- *can't have* to talk about things you feel sure haven't happened.
  It can't have been good news.

---

6 Use *must have*, *might have* and *can't have* to write a sentence about each of the people in the photos.

Reading

7 Read the following paragraph. Which of the following would be a good title for it?

Why people get depressed   **Language and emotions**   **Positive thinking**

People of all ages and from different cultures have far more words to express negative emotions, such as sadness, than they have to express positive emotions, such as happiness. When Professor Robert Schrauf of Penn State University asked people to make a list of adjectives expressing emotions, they wrote down words such as *happy, sad, angry, excited, afraid, anxious, surprised, depressed, grumpy, optimistic* and *satisfied*. The list showed that about half of all the words that people use to express emotions are negative, 30 per cent are positive and 20 per cent are neutral.

Speaking

8 Work in groups. Discuss the following question: Why do you think languages have more words for negative emotions than positive emotions?

Listening 5

9 Listen to the radio programme. In your discussion, did you come up with similar ideas?

10 Summarise the point of view expressed in the radio programme.

The reason that you hear more words for negative emotions than positive emotions is that ...

Problems and solutions

- 'A problem shared is a problem halved.' Do you agree?

Listening 6

1 Listen. What sort of radio programme is this?

2 Rewrite these sentences and phrases from the radio programme to explain what the phrasal verbs in italics mean.

1 I've *fallen out* with my best friend.
2 Tell her you want to *make up*.
3 Now, *cheer up!*
4 Now, just *calm down!*
5 It'll give you a chance to *catch up*.
6 Then you can *put this behind* you ...
7 ... and *move on*.

3 Listen again and answer the questions.

1 What have Justine, Tom and Rasheed got in common?
2 Why are they talking to Claudia?
3 What is Claudia's advice to Justine?
4 What is Claudia's advice to Tom?
5 What is Claudia's advice to Rasheed?
6 Who is in the most difficult situation, Justine, Tom or Rasheed?
7 What advice would you give them?

4 Listen one more time. Who says each of these sentences and what do they express?

1 *Claudia, g*

1 Oh, I see.
2 Why not? I've got nothing to lose.
3 What's on your mind?
4 I think you've done really well by phoning to talk about how you feel.
5 You can do it, I'm sure.
6 It's totally ridiculous!
7 No way! I'm really fed up about it.
8 It must have been hard to be told that.
9 I think it's really unfair!
10 You're right, it does sound unfair.
11 Go for it.
12 Thanks. OK, I will.

a acceptance
b encouragement
c frustration
d gratitude
e interest
f sympathy
g understanding

5 Complete the sentences with a suitable verb, using the present continuous with *always*.

1 They__ _____ _____ about their latest holiday but they never ask me about mine.
2 I__ _____ _____ my mobile phone. I can never find it.
3 He__ _____ _____ about the weather. Tell him to cheer up! It's not that bad.
4 You__ _____ _____ my bike without asking me. It's really annoying!
5 You__ _____ _____ . Just let me finish what I was saying for once!

Which two sentences are illustrated by the cartoons?

Speaking

6 Work in small groups. Think about a problem at home, at school or with your friends. It can be real or imaginary.

Make notes about the problem:

- What's the problem?
- How do you feel about it?
- When and where does it happen?
- Why do you think it happens?
- How long has it been going on?

Explain your problem to the other members of the group. They ask you questions and give you advice.

Use of English: Present continuous with *always*

This structure is used to describe annoying habits and to express criticism or self-criticism.

She's always talking about other people behind their backs, and I don't like it.

I'm always getting into trouble at school.

A

B

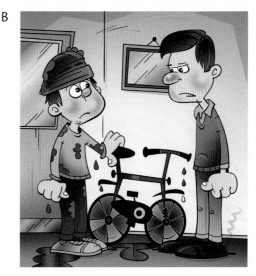

Beyond words

- What is non-verbal communication? Can you give some examples?

Reading

1 What is the purpose of this newspaper article?

International body language: a language with no words

Something as simple as a smile can display friendliness in one culture, embarrassment in another and impatience in a third. Even silence means different things in different places.

Gestures

The wrong gesture can lead to confusion or offence. Tapping your finger on the side of your head is a gesture to show memory in North America, but suggests insanity in Russia. Even nodding 'yes' or shaking one's head for 'no' can be misunderstood. In Turkey, for example, 'no' is expressed by a single upward movement of the head.

Silence

In North America and the UK, silence can be a problem. At work, at school or with friends, silence can make people feel uncomfortable. However, in other parts of the world, silence is not considered to be negative. In China, for example, silence can be used to show agreement and receptiveness. In many aboriginal cultures, a question will be answered only after a period of thoughtful silence.

Touch

Much of northern Europe is classed as a 'non-contact' culture, in which there's very little physical contact in people's daily interactions. Even accidentally brushing someone's arm requires an apology. By comparison, in the high-contact cultures of the Middle East, Latin America and southern Europe, physical touch is a big part of socialising.

What's more, there are different standards for who touches whom and where. In much of the Arab world, men hold hands and kiss each other in greeting, but would never do the same with a woman. In Thailand and Laos, it is taboo to touch someone's head, even if they're a child. In South Korea, older people can touch younger people with force when trying to get through a crowd, but younger people can't do the same.

Eye contact

In most western countries, frequent eye contact shows that you have confidence in someone and that you are interested in what they are saying. In many Middle Eastern countries, same-gender eye contact tends to be more sustained and intense than the western standard. In many Asian, African and Latin American countries, however, this unbroken eye contact would be considered aggressive and confrontational.

Based on an article by Anne Merritt in *The Daily Telegraph*, http://www.telegraph.co.uk/education/educationadvice/10055769/International-body-language-a-language-with-no-words.html

2 For each of the pictures, answer the question:
Where might this happen?

3 Try to complete these abstract nouns without looking at the text. Then check your answers.

1 friendli*ness*
2 embarrass_____
3 impati_____
4 confus_____
5 insan_____
6 receptive_____
7 confid_____

4 Write the adjectives which come from the nouns in Exercise 4.

1 *friendly*

Speaking

5 Work in pairs. In what kind of jobs is it important to know about the differences in non-verbal communication across different cultures and countries? Give your reasons. Make a list. Then compare as a class.

Project: Guide to non-verbal communication

6 Work in groups. Write a guide to non-verbal communication in your country for visitors of your own age. Use the article in Exercise 1 as a guide.

- Brainstorm ideas about what you will include in each of the following sections:
  Gestures
  Silence
  Touch
  Eye contact
- Write a draft of your guide.
- Check what you have written for spelling, punctuation and grammar.
- Write a final version.

4 The world of music

- **Topics** Taste in music; music and the emotions; musical instruments; the history of recorded sound
- **Use of English** Reported speech for present situations; question words as subjects and objects

What does music mean to you?

- When do you listen to music and why? What kind of music do you mainly listen to?

> I usually listen to music when I get home from school.

> I like music that's upbeat, – music that's energetic and positive, music that makes you feel happy.

> I like music that has a strong rhythm that makes you want to move.

> Some of my favourite songs are ballads. The lyrics can be quite sad but they express strong emotions.

> I mainly listen to music that's laid back. It makes me feel relaxed.

Reading

1 Read the article. Choose the sentence that summarises it best.

1 People prefer sad music to happy music.

2 Sad music can have a positive effect.

3 Everybody in the survey preferred classical music to other music.

Music and emotion

According to a recently published multi-national survey by the Free University of Berlin, sad music brings up 'a wide range of complex and partially positive emotions, such as nostalgia, peacefulness, tenderness, transcendence and wonder. People choose to listen to sad music especially when experiencing emotional distress or when feeling lonely.' It seems that the creative expression of sadness shows you that there is a way out of it.

Participants in the survey were asked to name their favourite piece of sad music. While their answers included a wide range of musical genres, the top three were: Beethoven's 'Moonlight Sonata', 'Moon Reflected in the Second Spring' by the Chinese composer Ah Bing and the American composer Samuel Barber's 'Adagio for Strings'.

Listening to sad music, it seems, can have beneficial effects. It provides consolation and helps to dispel negative moods.

Source: Pacific Standard

2 Match these abstract nouns from the text to their definitions. Use a dictionary to help you.

| nostalgia | peacefulness | tenderness | transcendence | wonder | distress | sadness | consolation |

a the feeling of being unhappy

b the feeling of being very unhappy and worried

c something that makes you feel better when you're sad or disappointed

d the feeling of being calm and quiet

e the feeling of going beyond the usual limits of something

f the gentle feeling of caring about someone you love

g great surprise and admiration when you see or experience something strange and new

h thoughts about happy times in the past

3 Which of the following statements are implied in the text?

1 The survey was answered by people from several different countries.

2 All the people who took part in the survey were musicians.

3 People were asked how they felt when they listened to sad music.

4 People tend to avoid listening to happy music when they're sad.

5 It wasn't only classical music that appeared in the list of favourite pieces of sad music.

Listening 7

4 Listen to the interviews. What do the three students interviewed all have in common?

Use of English: Reported speech and present situations

If you are reporting something which hasn't changed since the person said it, you don't need to change the tense of the verb.

Saskia said that music expresses a lot of the things she feels.

5 Read the Use of English box and complete the summaries. Listen again to check your answers.

1 Saskia said that sad songs _____ when she's a bit down.

2 She said it's important that a song _____.

3 Khalid said that music _____ sometimes.

4 He said that music _____ because he likes to move to music.

5 Rita said that playing the drums _____ .

6 She agreed that music _____ an important part in her life.

Speaking

6 Work in pairs. Ask each other: What does music mean to you?

I love music because ...

I listen to lots of ... because ...

If I'm a bit down / If I'm having a bad day ...

Music makes me feel ...

Music helps me to ...

Did you know?

For the International Day of Happiness, which was started in 2012, international figures are asked for their favourite song to put on the 'happiness playlist'. The Secretary General of the United Nations chose 'Signed, Sealed, Delivered, I'm Yours' by Stevie Wonder. What would you put on the playlist?

West meets East through music

- 'Music is the universal language of humanity.'
  Is this true?

Reading

1 Read about this orchestra. What is special about it?

The West-Eastern Divan Orchestra is a youth orchestra based in Seville, Spain. Its members are from, or have close family connections with, the Middle East or Spain. Every year, the orchestra advertises for young musicians to audition for its summer workshop and international tour which take place in July and August. To apply to join the orchestra, you need to be between 14 and 28 years old. (However, if an applicant is under 14 or over 28, they are sometimes considered if there are special circumstances.) In order to audition for the orchestra, applicants should send a video recording of themselves playing their instrument. The recording must be at least 10 minutes long.

Speaking

2 Work in pairs. Ask and answer questions about the orchestra.

1 Where ... ?
2 Who ... ?
3 When ... ?
4 How old ... ?
5 What ... ?

3 Work in small groups. Discuss these questions.

1 Why do you think the audition recording needs to be at least 10 minutes long?
2 Why do you think the applicants have to send a video and not just a sound recording?
3 Why do you think the orchestra might consider accepting musicians under the age of 14?
4 Why do you think musicians apply to play in the West-Eastern Divan Orchestra?

Reading

4 Read the advertisement for a new youth orchestra. How is this orchestra different from the West-Eastern Divan Orchestra?

Join The New National Youth Orchestra

Age
You should be between 13 and 21.

Auditions
You can audition in person or by sending a video recording of yourself playing two contrasting pieces. The recording should be between 6 and 10 minutes long.

Instruments
Violin, viola, cello, double bass, harp, flute, oboe, clarinet, bassoon, horn, trumpet, trombone, tuba and drums.

Availability
Successful applicants will be invited to a three-day workshop from 20th to 23rd July for rehearsals. After this, there will be a three-week tour of the country, playing at various music festivals and at a number of concert halls.

Vocabulary

5 Copy the chart and add the musical instruments mentioned in the advert to the correct sections.

Sections of the orchestra	Strings	Woodwind	Brass	Percussion
Instruments	harp			

Speaking

6 Work in small groups. You've been asked to be on the interview panel for the New National Youth Orchestra. What do you need to find out about each person? Write a list of questions to ask the applicants.

Remember:

- the musicians will have to be away from home for over three weeks
- they'll need to travel a lot
- they'll need to work long hours, practising and performing.

7 Take it in turns to ask other groups the questions you've written. The other groups must answer as if they were the applicants.

Writing

8 Find out about one of the instruments mentioned in your completed chart (Exercise 5). Write a short informative paragraph for a reference book. Include the following:

Where does it come from?

Which section of the orchestra does it belong to?

When were the first ones made?

What is it made of?

How big is it?

Are there different kinds?

Are there any famous performers of this instrument?

The sound of music

- Is music better live or when it's recorded? Why?

A brief history of recorded sound

1857	Édouard-Léon Scott de Martinville invented a device for recording sound. He called it the phonautograph. It traced the shape of sound waves on smoke-blackened paper or glass. The sound could not be played back. (However, in 2008, a group of researchers digitally converted the phonautograph recording of *Au clair de la lune* that de Martinville had made on 9 April 1860 and were able to play it. This is the earliest recording of the human voice.)
1878	Thomas Edison made a cylinder-based phonograph that he had invented the previous year. It could record and reproduce sound.
1887	Emile Berliner invented the gramophone. A year later he began to use flat discs rather than cylinders to record and play sound. By 1929, flat discs were so popular that cylinders were no longer used.
1904	The Italian opera singer, Enrico Caruso, became the first superstar recording artist and made over a million pounds (nearly 60 million pounds today) for his recordings.
1925	The invention of electrical recordings meant that microphones were used in studio sessions. Acoustic recordings became a thing of the past.
1931	In the very early days of cinema, the sound all came through one speaker. Alan Blumlein wanted to find a more realistic way of hearing the voices and sounds of a film so he invented stereo, which gave a wider field of sound.
1934	The first 'Talking Books' for the blind were introduced. They were recorded on gramophone records.
1948	Vinyl was used for making records, but it wasn't until 1964 that it became the standard material for making records.
1963	Cassettes were invented. It took about a decade before cassettes were widely bought by the general public.
1982	The first CD player was launched in Japan.
1998	The first portable media player (MP3) came onto the market in South Korea.
2000 to the present	With MP3s, you could listen to music downloaded from the Internet rather than buying CDs. However, vinyl records have not disappeared. In fact, they have become popular again and most new releases are produced on vinyl as well as being available as downloads and on CD. And with a digital audio workstation you can record, edit, mix and produce a whole album yourself.

Reading

1 Read the text.

Which pieces of information in the timeline do you find most surprising and why?

2 With a partner, answer the following questions.

1 What is stereo sound?

2 What are 'Talking Books'?

Speaking

3 Choose three items from the timeline to illustrate. In small groups, discuss and give reasons for your choices.

Use of English: Question words as subjects and objects

Question words as subjects	Question words as objects
When the question word is the subject of the question, we don't use an auxiliary verb:	When the question word is the object of the question, we use an auxiliary verb (*do, did*, etc):
Who invented the gramophone?	*Who do you associate with the invention of sound recording?*
Which came first, the phonograph or the gramophone?	*Which did people listen to in the 1970s, cassettes or CDs?*
What happened in 1982?	*What do Édouard-Léon Scott de Martinville and Thomas Edison have in common?*

Writing

4 Write questions using the prompts. Then answer them.

1 Which song / de Martinville / record in 1860?

2 Who / invent / the gramophone?

3 What / Emile Berliner / begin / to use in 1888?

4 Who / make / over £1 million from his recordings?

5 What / change / the way people heard sound in the cinema?

6 Which material / become / the standard for making records?

7 What / come / onto the market in 1998?

Project: Write a timeline

5 Research information on the history of the cinema or television and write a timeline, using *A brief history of recorded sound* as a model.

Find these time expressions in the text. Try to use them in your own timeline.

The previous year, ...

A year later, ...

By [1929], ...

In the very early days of [cinema], ...

It wasn't until [1964] that ...

It took [a decade] before ...

Autobiography

Playing with Flying Keys
Lang Lang

1 Read the text. Who is Lang Lang? Why do you think he's written an autobiography? Why do people write autobiographies?

2 Find these words in the text and try to understand their meaning from the context. Use a dictionary to check if you need to.

1 clutched *(line 2)*
2 wracked *(line 5)*
3 nightmares *(line 6)*
4 challenging *(line 10)*
5 gifted *(line 10)*
6 insisted *(line 11)*
7 eager *(line 12)*
8 prodigy *(line 20)*
9 dissuade *(line 23)*
10 accomplished *(line 26)*
11 scholarship *(line 32)*
12 anticipated *(line 39)*

3 Read the text and answer the questions.

1 This extract is the first part of the prologue to the book. What is the function of a prologue?
2 At the start of the extract, where is Lang Lang?
3 Who is with him?
4 What is about to happen?
5 How does he feel?
6 What is special about him?
7 What has his life been like so far?
8 How is his life about to change?

4 Work with a partner. Find these sentences in the text. Say what they mean.

1 'She had always been able to read my mind.'
2 'Your music will always keep you company.'
3 'My father had long believed I was destined for greatness.'
4 'The odds were against me.'
5 'I had only my talent to fall back on.'

Listening 8

5 Listen to more of the prologue. Do you think Lang Lang is going to get on the train to Beijing?

6 What facts do we learn from this part of the prologue? Think about the following:

1 Who is Lang Lang going to travel with?
2 Who will meet them and where?
3 Where will Lang Lang live and with whom?
4 Why will Lang Lang's mother go back to Shenyang?
5 What does Lang Lang's name mean?

7 Work in groups. Discuss these questions.

1 How would you describe Lang Lang's relationship with his mother and with his father?
2 What are the advantages and disadvantages of being a child prodigy?

Playing with Flying Keys

PROLOGUE

I was only nine years old, a third-grade student from the city of Shenyang, China, when I knew my life was going to change. I tightly clutched my mother's hand, waiting at the Shenyang station for the train to take us to Beijing, my new home. My father would be waiting for me. For the previous
5 forty-eight hours my body had been wracked by a high fever – every bone in my body ached – and in my nightmares monsters were chasing me. When the fever finally broke, my mother pronounced me fit enough to travel and helped me pack my suitcases.

   I had never been to Beijing, but I knew my life would soon be very
10 different, harder, more challenging. I was already a gifted young pianist, but my father insisted I move to Beijing to advance my musical skills. Part of me was eager to go; another part was incredibly sad. I would miss my friends, grandparents, and teachers in Shenyang. Most of all I would miss my mother. Still holding my hand, my mother, Xiulan, looked down at me
15 with her big brown eyes and beautiful smile. I was trying to appear brave, but she had always been able to read my mind. "Do not feel lonely or afraid, Lang Lang," she told me. "You are a very special boy. Your music will always keep you company."

   In Shenyang, I had been playing the piano since before I was two,
20 and many in my city considered me a prodigy. I had entered my first piano competition at age five. Newspapers had written stories about me and published my photo. My father had long believed I was destined for greatness, and nothing would dissuade him. But nothing would be easy either. In China in 1991, a nine-year-old pianist had little hope for a career
25 without attending the Beijing Conservatory and learning from the country's most accomplished teachers. This was my father's dream for me, and it had become mine as well.

   Admission to the conservatory was extremely competitive. Everyone had to play his or her best work for the judges. There were also written exams. I
30 would be competing against three thousand boys and girls my age from all over China. Only fifteen in my grade would be chosen for the conservatory and to win a financial scholarship, a necessity for my family, I would have to be in the top eight.

   The odds were against me. Since my father had quit his job to be with
35 me, my family was poor and lacked influence in the world of music. My piano teacher since I was four, a woman named Professor Zhu, did not have the power of teachers from bigger cities. To those at the conservatory, whose authority and power would determine my future, I was practically invisible. But my father, a clever man, had anticipated all this. To make
40 up for our disadvantages, he had ordered me to practise with incredible discipline since I was three years old. He knew that one day I would be competing against the best and brightest in a country of more than a billion people. I had only my talent to fall back on. I had to be prepared.

by Lang Lang

Review of Units 3–4

Vocabulary

Moods and feelings

1 Complete each sentence with the correct adjective.

> bored thrilled confused
> furious depressed apprehensive

1 I was really angry. In fact I was absolutely _____.

2 He was feeling a bit down, but he wasn't _____.

3 Rania's mum was delighted that Rania had passed her final music exam. 'I'm absolutely _____,' she said.

4 I wasn't really worried about starting at a new school. I was just a bit _____.

5 When you become a teenager you can feel mixed up at times and even quite _____.

6 I'm not in a bad mood. I'm just _____ because I've got nothing to do.

2 Choose the correct option.

1 The key to success is *confident / confidence*.

2 The changes in the timetable caused a lot of *confused / confusion* in the first week.

3 I wasn't hurt when I fell off the horse. I was just *embarrassed / embarrassment*.

4 We really appreciated their *friendly / friendliness* to us when we first arrived.

5 You need to calm down. Your *impatient / impatience* will get you into trouble one day.

6 It is often said that genius is close to *insane / insanity*.

7 She was such a good architect because she was always *receptive / receptiveness* to new ideas.

Musical instruments

3 Write the names of the musical instruments.

1 _____

2 *viola* _____

3 _____

4 _____

5 _____

Use of English

4 Chose the correct option.

1 It *must have / can't have* been easy to learn a new language in three months.

2 She *must have / might have* won the race if she hadn't fallen over in the last 50 metres.

3 You're much taller than when I last saw you. You *can't have / must have* grown a lot.

4 They *might have / can't have* got lost. I gave them very clear directions.

5 The violinist played the piece perfectly. She *can't have / must have* practised a lot before the concert.

5 Complete what these people are saying. Use the present continuous with *always*.

1 Don't criticise me so much. You*'re always criticising me.*

2 You've moved house three times in the last two years. You ____.

3 I've lost my mobile phone again. I ____.

4 Has she bought another new pair of shoes? She ____.

5 You shouldn't eat so much chocolate. You ____.

6 I wish our neighbours wouldn't play loud music every day. They ____.

6 Report what Anisa and Selim said. You don't need to change the tense of the verbs but you need to make sure they're in the correct form. You also need to change *I* to *she*, and so on.

I've got three brothers and one of them is married. I get on really well with my sister-in-law. We often go out together. I enjoy spending time with her.

Anisa

1 Anisa said *she's got three brothers and …*

I really like Maths and Science and my ambition is to be an engineer. I want to study at university in Canada because my elder brother lives there.

Selim

2 Selim said …

7 Write questions for the following answers about the New National Youth Orchestra.

1 Who / play **Who plays in the New National Youth Orchestra?**
Young international musicians between the ages of 13 and 21.

2 Who / contact
You contact the Audition Board if you want to audition in person.

3 What / happen
At the audition, you play a number of pieces and answer some questions.

4 What / send
You send a video recording if you can't audition in person.

5 Which / feature
Composers from Beethoven to Boulez feature in the programme.

6 Where / go
The orchestra goes to many different places.

General knowledge quiz

8 Work in pairs. Ask and answer the questions.

1 Which of these sentences is true?
 a Languages have more words for positive emotions than negative emotions.
 b Languages have more words for negative emotions than positive emotions.

2 Why do you have to be careful in Russia when you tap your finger on the side of your head?

3 Give an example of a country in which it is taboo to touch someone's head.

4 Listening to sad music can have beneficial effects. True or false?

5 Where is the West-Eastern Divan Orchestra based?

6 Where do the musicians in the West-Eastern Divan Orchestra come from?

7 When was the first recording of the human voice made, 1840, 1860 or 1925?

8 What did Emile Berliner invent?

9 Who was the first superstar recording artist?

10 What is the connection between vinyl and the history of recorded music?

- **Topics** Health, diet and exercise; illness and disease; discoveries in medicine
- **Use of English** Comparative adjectives and adverbs; prepositional and phrasal verbs; prepositional and adverbial time phrases

A game changer

- What do top sportspeople have to do in order to stay at the top of their game?

Reading

1 Read the review of *Serve to Win*. What kind of book is it: fiction, biography or autobiography?

Novak Djokovic is one of the top tennis players of all time.

But in his late teens, he had a crisis. And he's written a book about it.

Serve to Win by Novak Djokovic

He was playing in a tournament and he collapsed on court. He didn't know what the problem was, but as he says: 'All I could hear was roaring in my head. All I could feel was pain and it felt as if someone had poured concrete into my legs. Just as I was reaching for the top, I hit the bottom.'

He changed the type of trainers he wore and he changed his coach. He even moved his training camp to Abu Dhabi because he thought that by practising in the heat he would be better prepared on court. But he was still having problems. He just couldn't keep up. 'Physically I couldn't compete' he says. 'Mentally I didn't feel I belonged on the same court as the best players in the game. There was something about me that was broken, unhealthy, unfit.'

In early 2010, a doctor told him that he could help him. He needed to change his diet. Up until then, he'd enjoyed pizza, pasta and bread from his parents' restaurant as well as heavy red meat dishes. And, as he admits, 'I also snacked on candy bars and other sugary foods during matches, thinking they would help to keep my energy up.' The doctor advised him to give up eating all those things and to replace them with foods such as brown rice, fruit and leafy green vegetables. It wasn't just a question of cutting down on bread, pasta and pizza. He had to cut them out of his diet altogether.

As Djokovic says in the book: 'I had to learn to listen to my body. Once I did, everything changed. I feel fresher, more alert and more energetic than I have in my life.' His friends, too, noticed how his moods and energy levels were more in balance. He was less anxious, more focused and less likely to get angry when things were not going well on court.

I wouldn't normally be interested in reading about a sports personality.

And I don't enjoy biographies of celebrities. But this book is different. It's not full of accounts of how I won this, and how much training I did for that and how wonderful I am. It's a very moving and personal account of how Djokovic solved a problem which was affecting his whole life.

2 Answer these questions.

1 How did Djokovic realise that something was wrong?
2 At first, what did he do to try to solve the problem?
3 What did Djokovic realise after his visit to the doctor?
4 What was the effect of the changes the doctor suggested?
5 Why has the reviewer chosen to review this book?

3 Work in pairs. Find the words in column A in the review. Then discuss the differences between them and the words in column B.

A	B
1 collapsed	fell down
2 pain	illness
3 unhealthy	ill
4 unfit	unwell
5 alert	lively
6 energetic	determined
7 anxious	angry

Use of English: Prepositional and phrasal verbs

Prepositional and phrasal verbs are verbs which are followed by one or more small words like *on, out, up* and so on. The meaning of these verbs is sometimes very different from the meaning of the parts taken separately.

cut down on   keep up
cut out   snack on
give up

4 Use the verbs in the Use of English box to complete the sentences.

1 My grandfather ___ playing football when he was 70 but he still plays tennis.
2 If you feel hungry between meals it's better to ___ fruit than on chocolate bars.
3 It's great that you enjoy swimming so much but you need to ___ the time you spend training if you're feeling tired at school.
4 I've decided to ___ sweets and sugary drinks altogether. After all, you don't need them.
5 My younger sister is a really good runner. She can ___ with people three years older than her.

Speaking

5 Work in pairs. Ask and answer questions about Novak Djokovic.

A What happened to Novak Djokovic in his late teens?
B He had a crisis. He was playing ...

Writing

6 Write a summary of Djokovic's story in under 100 words.
Use these prompts to help you:

While he was playing in a tournament, ...

He didn't know ...

He tried ...

Then, in 2010, ...

He gave up ...

The result was that ...

Food for thought

● What helps you to be healthy?

Time for fitness

Speaking

1 Work in pairs. Discuss the questions. Then share your ideas with the class.

1 Do you think there's a link between eating regular meals and being able to concentrate in class?

2 Which is the most important meal of the day and why?

3 Why do some people get impatient or bad-tempered when they're hungry?

4 The more exercise you do, the better you feel. Do you think this is true?

Reading

2 Read the extracts from a magazine article about staying healthy. Choose a title for each extract.

a The importance of eating regularly

b The connection between food and sleeping well

c The benefits of exercise

d The link between exercise and intelligence

Language tip

Although the words *likely* and *unlikely* end in *–ly*, they are adjectives, not adverbs.

Note how you use these words:
You're likely to eat more calories.
NOT: ~~It's likely for you to eat more calories.~~

1

According to Dr Brian Stollery of Bristol University, 'Skipping meals leads to low blood sugar, which affects our mood and our ability to think clearly. Our brains use about 20% of the energy used by our bodies. ... We need to keep up a steady supply of energy so that the brain can do its job.' It is particularly important to eat a good carbohydrate-based breakfast to restore blood sugar levels after a night's sleep. You also need to eat regular meals during the day because if you don't, the level of serotonin in your body drops. Serotonin is the chemical that helps to keep your moods and emotions in balance.

There is another consequence of skipping meals: you're likely to eat more calories. If you don't eat regularly, your blood sugar levels drop, so you crave sweet, carbohydrate-rich snacks, full of calories. Eating a lot of these snacks can lead to serious health problems such as diabetes or heart disease.

2

Studies have found that people who do sport in their free time appear to be healthier and catch coughs and colds less frequently than people who are less active. Moderate exercise helps the immune cells to circulate around the body more quickly and therefore helps to kill bacteria and viruses more efficiently. However, there is also evidence that too much exercise can have the opposite effect. It can suppress the immune system, especially after extreme exercise, making the body more susceptible to illness and less able to fight off disease.

A further point to remember is that if you are ill, you should not exercise too much because your body is already working hard to fight the infection. Putting stress on your system will mean that your recovery is likely to be slower.

3 Match the words with their definitions.

1	skipping	**a**	likely to be affected by something
2	restore	**b**	not doing something that you usually do or should do
3	crave	**c**	stop something working properly
4	suppress	**d**	make something exist again
5	susceptible	**e**	want something very much

4 Can you work out the meaning of these medical words from the context?
Check in a dictionary if you need to. Are any of the words similar in your language?

1	diabetes	**3**	cells	**5**	viruses	**7**	infection
2	immune system	**4**	bacteria	**6**	disease	**8**	recovery

Use of English: Comparative adjectives and adverbs

To make **comparative adjectives**, add *(e)r* to the adjective or use *more* in front of the adjective. To make **negative comparisons**, use *less* in front of the adjective.	*Your recovery is likely to be slower.* *Too much exercise makes the body more susceptible to illness and less able to fight off disease.*
To make **comparative adverbs**, use *more* and add *–ly* to the adjective. To make **negative comparisons**, use *less* in front of the adverb.	*Moderate exercise helps the immune cells to circulate around the body more quickly.* *Moderate exercise helps to kill bacteria and viruses more efficiently.* *Active people catch coughs and colds less frequently.*

The rules for forming comparative adjectives and a list of irregular adverbs are given on page 114 of the Workbook.

5 Make comparative adjectives or adverbs from the words in the box to complete the sentences. Use each word once only.

> tired   clear   slow   efficient   likely   strong

1 Potatoes, rice and pasta release energy into the body much ***more slowly*** than sweet snacks.
2 Students who come to school without having had breakfast work _____ during the morning.
3 I wear contact lenses when I play tennis because I can see _____ with them.
4 People who do regular exercise have a _____ immune system.
5 I've started going to bed earlier and I've noticed I'm much _____ at school the next day.
6 You're _____ to have mood swings if you're hungry.

Speaking

6 Look again at the questions in Exercise 1. Continue your discussion using the information in the article.

The story of vaccination

● Which are the most important discoveries in medicine?

Reading and speaking

1 Work in pairs.
Partner A: Read *Lady Mary's campaign against smallpox*.
Partner B: Read *From country doctor to medical pioneer*.

2 In the same pairs, with your books closed, tell your partner about Lady Mary / Edward Jenner.

Your partner can ask questions to find out more and to check that he / she understands:

How old were the children?

You said Jenner carried out an 'experience'. Do you mean an 'experiment'?

Listening 9

3 Listen to a presentation about Edward Jenner. Four pieces of information are wrong. Put your hand up when you hear something you think is wrong.

4 Listen again. Compare what Victor says with the text about Edward Jenner. What are the four pieces of information that Victor gets wrong?

Use of English: Prepositional and adverbial time phrases

Time phrases are useful when you're writing a narrative or giving biographical details. They go at the beginning or the end of a sentence.

In 1716	Two months later
During her time in Constantinople	Shortly afterwards
After leaving prison	Over a century later
By 1853	At first

5 Complete the time phrases in these sentences.

1 Louis Pasteur was born in France ____ 1822.

2 ____ his early years he was an average student.

3 He took the university entrance exam in1842 but he failed. Two years ____ he passed the exam.

4 ____ 1848 he had become Professor of Chemistry at the University of Strasbourg.

5 Shortly ____, in 1849, he married Marie Laurent. They had five children.

Project: Write a profile of a medical pioneer

6 Work in small groups. Find out more about Louis Pasteur or another famous medical pioneer.
Write a short entry for a reference book about their contribution to medical history.

● Divide the work among the members of the group.
● Find out:
    1 when and where the person you have chosen lived
    2 how they made their discovery
    3 how the discovery was received at the time
    4 how the discovery helped people.

● Use these four headings to write four paragraphs about the person you've chosen. Remember to use time phrases, such as the ones in the Use of English box.

● Find pictures to illustrate your profile.

Lady Mary's campaign against smallpox

Lady Mary Wortley Montagu (1689–1762) was born in London. In 1716 she went with her husband, the British Ambassador, to Turkey. During her time in Constantinople (now Istanbul), she saw how children were protected from smallpox, a common and often fatal disease of the time. Infected material taken from somebody with smallpox was rubbed into scratches made on the children's arms. Although afterwards the children were with people who had the disease, they didn't catch it. She was so impressed that she asked her doctor to do the same for her 5-year-old son and 4-year-old daughter.

When Lady Mary returned to England, she persuaded doctors to test the method on six prisoners who were promised their freedom if they agreed. All the prisoners survived and were released. After leaving prison, one was exposed to two children with smallpox and he was found to be immune to the disease. After the two daughters of the Prince of Wales were inoculated, the process became widely used in Britain. But despite the success of inoculation, there were still risks. First, because inoculating with too little of the infected material did nothing, while too much overwhelmed the immune system. Second, inoculated people were temporarily carriers of smallpox and could infect others. It wasn't until Edward Jenner's use of cowpox to inoculate people against smallpox that the process became safe, providing immunity without risk of infection.

From country doctor to medical pioneer

As a boy, Edward Jenner (1749–1823) had been inoculated against smallpox, using the method promoted by Lady Mary. When he became a doctor, he inoculated his own patients against the disease, despite being aware of the risks.

Jenner sometimes treated milkmaids, girls who looked after cows, for cowpox. Cowpox was similar to smallpox but not serious or fatal. He noticed that the girls who had had cowpox never got smallpox. In 1796, he carried out an experiment on an 8-year-old boy called James Phipps. He took infected material from a milkmaid with cowpox and inoculated James with it. Two months later, Jenner inoculated James with smallpox. The boy didn't get the disease.

This new process, using cowpox, was much safer than inoculating people with smallpox. Jenner even tested the process on his 11-month-old son. Shortly afterwards, in 1798, Jenner published the results of his work. At first, his discovery of 'vaccination', as he and his colleagues called it, was criticised and even laughed at. Cartoons appeared in newspapers showing people with cows' heads after he had vaccinated them.

However, by 1853, 30 years after Jenner's death, vaccination against smallpox had become compulsory throughout Britain. Just over a century later, in 1980, the World Health Organization declared that smallpox had been eradicated.

fatal resulting in death
scratches thin cuts on the surface of the skin

inoculated given a weak form of a disease, usually with a needle, to protect against the disease
overwhelmed had an effect that was too strong to fight against

carriers people who pass a disease to other people without having it themselves
patients people a doctor looks after
eradicated completely removed

Did you know?

The word 'vaccination' comes from the Latin word 'vacca' for 'cow'. At first, vaccination referred only to inoculation against smallpox but in 1881, the French chemist Louis Pasteur proposed that the word should be used for inoculations against all diseases, in honour of the work done by Jenner.

6 Leisure time

- **Topics** Leisure interests, use of digital communication and media; social media; sleep and health

- **Use of English** Pronouns expressing quantity in short answers (*none, hardly any*, etc.); verbs followed by the *-ing* form; position of adverbs *just, so, really*

Leisure for pleasure

- Why do people become 'fans' of a particular sport or leisure activity?

Speaking

1 Work in pairs. Find out about your partner's leisure activities. Ask questions beginning with the following words and phrases:
How much time ... ? How often ... ? How many ... ? Do you ever ...?

> How much time do you spend watching football on TV?

> Do you ever wake up in the night to check for messages on your mobile phone?

> How many books have you read in the last month?

Language tip

In English there are a number of colloquial expressions to describe people who have a strong interest in particular leisure activities; for example, *a football fan, a bookworm, a film buff, a fitness fanatic, a social networker, a music lover.*

2 What are the most popular leisure activities in your class? Share with the class what you found out about your partner in Exercise 1. Draw conclusions, like this:
There are a lot of film buffs in our class.
There aren't many bookworms.

3 The survey on page 47 relates to German teenagers. Study it and answer the questions.

1 What does the survey tell you about the differences between boys and girls?
It shows that more girls than boys... but fewer girls ...

2 Do any of the findings in the survey surprise you?
It surprises me that ...

3 What would you expect if you did a similar survey in your class?
I think that if we did a similar survey, we'd find that ...

Use of English: Pronouns expressing quantity in short answers

You can use the following expressions as short answers without nouns, if the meaning is clear.

none (of them)	Q: How many adults took part in this survey?
very few	
very little	A: *None.*
not much	Q: How many of the boys in the survey read e-books?
hardly any	
not (that) many	
quite a few	A: *Very few. / Hardly any.*
a lot	Q: Which devices are important for German teenagers: mobile phones or MP3 players?
plenty	
loads	
(almost) all of them	
For talking about two things:	A: *Both.* (Rather than 'Both mobile phones and MP3 players'.)
both	
neither	

Which of these devices or types of media do you use daily or several times a week?

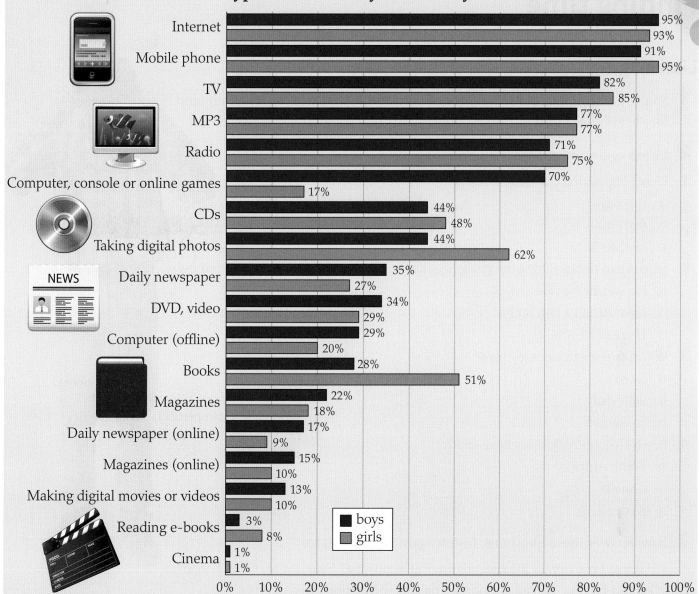

Internet — 95% / 93%
Mobile phone — 91% / 95%
TV — 82% / 85%
MP3 — 77% / 77%
Radio — 71% / 75%
Computer, console or online games — 70% / 17%
CDs — 44% / 48%
Taking digital photos — 44% / 62%
Daily newspaper — 35% / 27%
DVD, video — 34% / 29%
Computer (offline) — 29% / 20%
Books — 28% / 51%
Magazines — 22% / 18%
Daily newspaper (online) — 17% / 9%
Magazines (online) — 15% / 10%
Making digital movies or videos — 13% / 10%
Reading e-books — 3% / 8%
Cinema — 1% / 1%

■ boys
■ girls

0% 10% 20% 30% 40% 50% 60% 70% 80% 90% 100%

4 Answer these questions about the teenagers in the survey. Use the expressions from the Use of English box.

1 How many German teenagers use a mobile phone daily or several times a week?
2 How many texts are sent and how many phone calls do you think are made every day by German teenagers?
3 Who listens to music on an MP3 player – boys or girls?
4 How many girls play computer games?
5 How many teenagers take digital photos?
6 How many boys read books?
7 How many teenagers go to the cinema?

5 Conduct your own survey about devices and types of media in your class. Record your results in a bar chart.

Finding time

● Can you always find something to do in your free time? Give examples.

Listening 🔟

1 You're going to hear Jay talking about a challenge that his school set him and his classmates. What was the challenge?

2 Listen again and choose the correct answers.

1 How long did the challenge last?
   a two days
   b five days
   c one week

2 Jay did two things during the challenge that he didn't usually do. What were they?
   a He watched a video.
   b He watched a film on TV.
   c He read a book.

3 Which two sports does Jay play?
   a football
   b volleyball
   c basketball

4 In which country does Jay have family?
   a South Africa
   b Canada
   c Kenya

3 Now answer these questions. Listen again if you need to.

1 What was Jay's view of the challenge at the beginning? How did his view change?
2 What did Jay find difficult during the challenge? Mention three things.
3 What did he learn from the challenge?

Speaking

4 Work in pairs. How would you feel if you couldn't use your mobile or any social media for a week?

I think I'd feel a bit …
I'd miss …
I wouldn't be able to …
But I'd probably …

Use of English: Verbs followed by the *-ing* form

Remember that some verbs are followed by the *-ing* form.

miss	*I missed being in contact with my friends.*
spend time	*I spent the usual amount of time doing my homework.*
waste time	*I don't think I waste time going online, checking my messages, texting and so on.*
fancy	*I fancied meeting up with friends to play basketball.*
feel like	*I felt like giving up.*

Other verbs that are followed by the *-ing* form include:
like, love, enjoy, prefer, don't mind, dislike, hate, can't face, can't stand.

5 Complete the sentences using an *-ing* form to make them true for you.

1 I spend quite a lot of time …

2 I sometimes waste time …

3 Next weekend, I fancy …

4 I don't mind … but I hate …

5 When I'm really tired I can't face …

6 I enjoy … but I prefer …

Reading

6 Read what three teenagers say about how they spend their free time. What do they have in common?

 FootballFan

I sometimes play football after school but I'd really like to play for a team. The problem is, I just don't have time because I'd have to go to training sessions and team practice. With all the homework we have to do I couldn't fit it in.

 BlueSkyCalm

I really enjoy listening to music but I'd love to play an instrument like the piano or the guitar. I just wish I had more time so that I could have lessons. I'd love to learn to ride too but I can't afford riding lessons – they're so expensive.

 TechnoKid

My parents say I spend too much time playing video games and on social media. But I still get all my homework done. It's true I'd like to do more outdoor stuff but it's hard to find the time. The good thing is, I'm never bored.

7 Rewrite this passage adding *just*, *really* and *still* to give emphasis where appropriate. Use each word once.

My friend Malik is amazing. He's good at all his school subjects and he's brilliant at sport. He spends a lot of time helping his parents in their shop and he manages to get all his homework done on time. I don't know how he does it!

Use of English: Adverbs *just*, *really*, *still*

You can use *just*, *really* and *still* to add emphasis to what you're saying.
I just wish I had more time.
I still get all my homework done.
I really enjoy listening to music.

In negative sentences, adverbs usually come before *not* if they emphasise the negative:
I just don't have time.
I still haven't had time to watch the TV series I recorded.
I really don't have time to do all the things I'd like to do.

Writing

8 Write two lists:

What I do in my free time   What I'd like to do in my free time

Use your lists to write a comment for the website, like the ones in Exercise 6.

Try to include verbs followed by the *-ing* form and the adverbs *just*, *really* and *still*.

A good night's sleep

- Are you an early bird or a night owl?

Reading

1 Sometimes writers use their writing to tell you what they believe. Their writing has 'a message'. What is the message of this newspaper article?

Average person now spends more time on their phone and laptop than *SLEEPING*, study claims

Do you text late into the night and reach for your phone as soon as you wake up?

Many adults now spend more hours of the day using laptops and phones than they do asleep, a survey has revealed.

People spend an average of 8 hours 21 minutes sleeping a day – but spend an average of 8 hours 41 minutes on media devices.

The majority (81 per cent) of smartphone users have their phones switched on all the time, even in bed, they said.

And four in ten adults and teenagers said there had been occasions when they checked their smartphone in the night after it woke them up.

They also spend more time each morning checking emails and using the internet than eating breakfast or taking care of their appearance.

Experts have warned that this means that people are not getting enough quality sleep, which has a direct effect on their health.

They have warned that over time, a continued lack of sleep can lead to a weakened immune system and an increased risk of heart disease, high blood pressure and diabetes.

It can also make a person more susceptible to mental health problems such as anxiety and depression.

Dr Nerina Ramlakhan, a sleep and energy coach, advises turning off all technological devices at least 60–90 minutes before going to sleep in order to give the mind time to wind down.

And it's not just adults who are at risk. A recent focus group of almost 500 students aged 13–15, held by Dr Ramlakhan, showed cause for concern, as an alarming number complained of sleep problems and feeling exhausted.

Of those who complained, almost 80 per cent were using electronic devices in bed.

She advises keeping the bedroom tech-free to avoid future health issues.

She said: 'Your bedroom is one of the most important factors when it comes to getting a great night's sleep. Banishing technology from the bedroom is one of the easiest things people can do to promote a relaxing sleep environment and ensure they're getting enough rest for the body to recover overnight.'

Source: The Daily Mail

2 Match these words and phrases from the article with their meanings.

1	taking care of their appearance	a	very tired
2	wind down	b	encourage or help something to develop
3	at risk	c	gradually relax
4	focus group	d	in danger
5	cause for concern	e	making sure they look good
6	exhausted	f	not allowing someone or something to stay in a particular place
7	banishing	g	reason to be worried
8	promote	h	a small number of people brought together to discuss a particular subject in order to solve a problem or suggest ideas

3 Refer to the newspaper article to complete the following sentences. Then number the sentences in the correct order to create a summary of the article.

a Experts advise making the _____ a 'tech-free' zone in order to boost rest.

b _____ in ten smartphone users check their phone in the night if it wakes them.

c More time is spent checking emails in the morning than eating _____ .

d Experts warn constant exposure to devices is leading to poor _____ .

e The average person spends _____ hours and 41 minutes on electronic devices.

f This is 20 minutes _____ than the average night's sleep, it is claimed.

4 Answer these questions.

1 How many of the people who were questioned for the survey said they never switched their smartphone off?

2 What are the dangers of letting technology interrupt your sleep?

3 What should you do to prepare for a good night's sleep?

4 What problems did the students in the focus group have?

5 What should you avoid having in the bedroom, according to the article?

Project: Design and write a poster

5 Use these headings to create a poster promoting a healthy lifestyle for teenagers.

- Regular meals
- Moderate exercise
- Making the most of your free time
- A healthy diet
- Getting enough sleep

1 Work in small groups. Brainstorm ideas for each section of the poster.

2 Write a draft. You need a short informative paragraph for each section.

3 Find illustrations for your poster and design it using your draft text.

4 Check your text carefully for spelling, grammar and punctuation.

5 Produce the final version of your poster.

> **Be at the top of your game!**

Poetry ⑪

Haiku

1 Read about haiku. What are the essential elements of a haiku? Write a series of bullet points.

- It's short.

> Haiku is a form of poetry that became popular in Japan in the seventeenth century, particularly through the work of Matsuo Bashō (1644–94). In Japanese, haiku poems traditionally appear in a single vertical line and the idea is to say them in one breath. Why? Because a haiku aims to capture a moment in time, and a moment is short.
>
> A haiku makes you notice something, which is why there is often an element of surprise, but not of shock, because the overriding emotion is of sympathy and understanding. There are usually one or two images in a haiku, especially images from nature, and there is often a reference to a season. (Japan has four seasons: spring, summer, autumn and winter.)

2 Read the translation of a well-known haiku and the notes about it. Why do you think haiku poems are popular?

	Notes:
Old pond leap-splash – a frog.	The translator has used long-sounding vowels to give the impression of time standing still in this reference to nature.
	Suddenly there is movement (*leap*) and sound (*splash*). This is the element of surprise.
Matsuo Bashō	The image of the frog leaping and splashing contrasts with the silent stillness of the old pond. The poet is noticing the importance of a small creature in the wider world of the pond.

3 Read some more haiku poems by Matsuo Bashō translated into English and answer these questions.

1 What visual images does the poet create in each haiku?

2 What are the elements of surprise and contrast in each one?

3 What emotion does each one express?

4 Which seasons are referred to?

Friends part
for ever – wild geese
lost in cloud.

Wake, butterfly –
it's late, we've miles
to go together.

Violets –
how precious on
a mountain path.

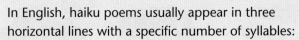

In English, haiku poems usually appear in three horizontal lines with a specific number of syllables:

line 1   5 syllables
line 2   7 syllables
line 3   5 syllables

Total = 17 syllables

4 Here are some haiku poems written in English. As you read them, count out the syllables in each line.

Haikus

Swaying in the breeze,
Their heads nodding, bluebells ring,
Heralding summer.

Grey as steel, the sea
Shimmers in the fading light:
Day slides into night.

John Foster

Summer haiku

Shimmering heat-waves –
A hot pebble in the hand,
Light-dance on the sea.

Wendy Cope

swaying moving slowly from side to side
bluebells spring plants with blue flowers shaped like a bell
heralding announcing that something is going to happen
steel a strong metal made from iron and carbon
shimmers shines with a soft light that looks as if it shakes slightly

5 Work in pairs. Discuss the haiku poems in Exercise 4 using the questions in Exercise 3.

6 Read these humorous haiku poems and answer the questions.

NoHaiku

I'm sorry to say
that I really don't feel like
a haiku today.

Adrian Henri

1 Why is the title of this poem 'NoHaiku'? Say it quickly and you'll get the answer! (It's something you say to decline an offer or an invitation politely.)

Lowku Haiku

If a poem has
Just sixteen syllables
Is it a lowku?

Roger Stevens

2 The title of this poem, 'Lowku Haiku', is a play on words. What is a 'play on words'?

Haiku

To convey one's mood
in seventeen syllables
is very diffic

John Cooper Clarke

3 Why hasn't the poet finished this haiku?

7 Write your own haiku. It can be serious or humorous.

Review of Units 5–6

Vocabulary

Health and fitness

1 Choose the correct option.

1 He felt a sharp *pain / illness* in his leg.
2 He lost his balance and *fell down / collapsed* the stairs.
3 I'm quite *unfit / unwell* at the moment so I'll have to train hard to be ready for the tournament.
4 You need to be *alert / lively* in class so remember to eat a good breakfast.
5 You'll feel more *determined / energetic* if you have a balanced diet.

2 Match the medical words to their definitions.

1 bacteria
2 cell
3 diabetes
4 immune
5 infection
6 inoculation
7 recovery

a an illness in which the body cannot control the level of sugar in the blood
b protected against a disease
c the smallest living part of an animal or a plant
d very small living things which sometimes cause disease
e a disease in part of your body that is caused by bacteria or a virus
f when you feel better again after an illness
g giving a weak form of a disease, usually by injection, to protect against that disease

Leisure time

3 Complete the expressions and match them to the pictures.

1 bookw_____   4 football f_____
2 film b_____   5 music l_____
3 fitness f_____   6 social n_____

Use of English

4 Complete the sentences.

My plans for a healthier lifestyle

1 I need to cut down _____ sugar in my diet.
2 I'm trying to cut _____ sweets altogether.
3 I need to keep my energy levels _____ because I do a lot of sport.
4 I'm going to snack _____ fruit and nuts rather than biscuits.
5 But I'm not going to give _____ chocolate!

5 Choose the correct option.

1 You catch coughs and colds *less frequently / less frequent* if you're an active person.
2 If you don't stay in bed when you've got flu, your recovery is likely to be *slower / more slowly*.
3 If you do regular exercise, your heart works *more efficient / more efficiently*.
4 Exercise helps the immune cells to circulate round the body *quicker / more quickly*.
5 If you were *more active / more actively*, I'm sure you'd feel better.

6 Complete the text with the correct words. Use each word once only.

| after | by | during | in | later | afterwards |

Alexander Fleming was born in Scotland _____[1] 1881. He studied medicine in London and _____[2] his time at St Mary's Hospital Medical School, he won the gold medal as the top medical student. That was in 1908. He served as an army doctor in World War 1. _____[3] leaving the army at the end of the war in 1918, he returned to St Mary's and ten years _____[4] he was elected Professor of the Medical School. Shortly _____[5], while working on the influenza virus, he discovered penicillin – the first antibiotic. _____[6] 1945, he had won many awards, including the Nobel Prize for Medicine.

7 Choose the correct answer for each question. Use each word or phrase once only.

| Both | Loads | None of them |
| Very little | Hardly any | |

1 A: You're always texting. How many texts do you send every day?

B:

2 A: How many teenagers like getting up early?

B:

3 A: Which do you use every day, a smartphone or a laptop?

B:

4 A: How much TV do you watch?

B:

5 A: How many of the students in your class read a newspaper every day?

B:

8 Put the words in the correct places in the sentences.

1 I love listening to music while I'm reading. (*really*)

2 I've been learning French for three years but I can't say very much. (*still*)

3 I wish I hadn't wasted time. (*just*)

4 I don't understand how people can spend all day at the beach. (*just*)

5 Ugh! Horrible! I don't like that cheese. (*really*)

6 I haven't been able to watch all the programmes I've recorded. (*still*)

General knowledge quiz

9 Work in pairs. Ask and answer the questions.

1 What sport does Novak Djokovic play?

2 What is the title of Novak Djokovic's autobiography?

3 What was the major change Djokovic made to his lifestyle in 2010?

4 What is a virus?

5 What is the name of the chemical which helps to keep your moods and emotions in balance?

6 In which country did Lady Mary Wortley Montagu see children being protected from a disease which was often fatal?

7 What did Edward Jenner discover?

8 When was smallpox eradicated from the world? Was it 1880, 1920 or 1980?

9 Explain the origin of the word 'vaccination'.

10 How long does the average person spend sleeping? Is it 6 hours 21 minutes, 7 hours 21 minutes or 8 hours 21 minutes?

- **Topics** Renewable and non-renewable sources of energy; energy efficiency
- **Use of English** Determiners and pre-determiners (*some of the beaches*); compound adjectives; future continuous

A tropical paradise

- Where is Costa Rica? Why do you think people call it a tropical paradise?

Listening 12

1 Listen to a radio programme about energy resources in Costa Rica. What does the picture show? What do you think it has to do with the programme?

Note: *Carbon-neutral* means that you don't produce more CO_2 than you can absorb.

2 Work in pairs. Listen again. What do these numbers refer to?

1 4.8 million   *The population of Costa Rica.*
2 124
3 25%
4 within ten years

5 88%
6 68%
7 15%

3 Write a sentence including each of the numbers in Exercise 2.

1 *The population of Costa Rica is 4.8 million.*

4 Work in groups. Discuss these questions.

1 What makes Costa Rica a good destination for tourists?

2 In the radio programme, Samira says: 'So it's a very green country – in more ways than one.' What does she mean?

3 Could other countries follow the model of Costa Rica with regard to energy provision?

Use of English: Determiners and pre-determiners

Determiners are words like *the, a / an, this, some, every*. You usually have one determiner before a noun or noun phrase:

some beautiful beaches
most people

You can combine determiners to be more specific or to give emphasis. The first determiner is called a 'pre-determiner'. Note that you need to use *of* in the following expressions:

Some of the beaches were fantastic for swimming.

Every one of the beaches had something special.

In Costa Rica, most of the volcanoes are inactive.

Each of the six active volcanoes is a source of geothermal power.

Which of these energy sources are renewable?

Neither of my parents speaks Spanish.

Remember that *another* is written as one word, NOT ~~an other~~.

The country has another major natural energy source: volcanoes.

Remember that *such* comes before the article *a / an*:

Why is Costa Rica such an attractive place?

---

5 Add *of* where necessary in these sentences.

1 Some ___ the new buildings in our city have solar panels.

2 Each ___ the leisure centres in our town has a swimming pool.

3 In 20 years' time most ___ cars will be electric.

4 Our house is powered by solar energy most ___ the time.

5 Most ___ days I try to walk or cycle to school.

6 Neither ___ my parents has been to Costa Rica.

Writing

6 Use the following information to write about Sweden. Use the sentences you've written in Exercise 3 as a model.

SWEDEN FACT FILE

1 Population 9.8 million

2 29 national parks + protected areas = 11 per cent of total land area

3 carbon neutral by 2050

4 48 per cent energy production from renewable sources

5 95 per cent renewable energy from hydroelectric plants.

Did you know?

In summer, the far north of Sweden has 24 hours of daylight for 56 days.

But in winter it has 32 days when it doesn't get light.

How would you feel about living there?

What does it mean to be green?

- What do you associate with the colour green?

Reading

1 Work in pairs. Take turns to ask and answer the questions in the quiz.

How green are you?

1 How many eco-friendly products have you got, e.g. a solar-powered charger for your mobile phone?
  a none
  b one
  c more than one

2 What do you think about agreeing to spend no more than two minutes in the shower, in order to save water?
  a No way!
  b I'll think about it.
  c That's a good idea.

3 What does a biomass generator do?
  a I haven't got a clue.
  b I think it produces energy, but I'm not sure how.
  c It converts plant material into energy.

4 What is a low-energy light bulb?
  a One that doesn't last very long.
  b One that doesn't give much light.
  c It's longer-lasting and doesn't use as much electricity as other light bulbs.

5 In energy terms, what makes a car 'green'?
  a It's painted green so it blends in with the countryside.
  b Its size – it's a very small car for just two people.
  c It doesn't produce much CO_2 because it's powered wholly or partly by electricity instead of petrol or diesel.

6 Which of these applies to you?
  a I don't understand why people switch lights off. It's better just to leave them on.
  b I usually put my laptop into sleep mode when I'm not using it.
  c I switch things off when I'm not using them because I don't want to waste electricity.

7 Is your home energy-efficient?
  a I don't know. What does 'energy-efficient' mean?
  b I think we use low-energy light bulbs.
  c Most of the power is supplied by solar cells and we're careful not to waste electricity.

Answers

Mostly a
Green isn't your favourite colour, is it?

Mostly b
You're definitely eco-aware.

Mostly c
You clearly care about the environment and the future of the planet.

Vocabulary

2 Work in pairs. Find these compound adjectives in the quiz and explain what they mean.

1 eco-friendly
2 solar-powered
3 low-energy
4 longer-lasting
5 energy-efficient

3 Work in small groups. Discuss these two questions.

1 What do you do in your daily life to be eco-friendly?
2 What are the difficulties for you in being totally eco-friendly?

4 Write a summary of the answers to the questions in Exercise 3.

Some of the people in our group have solar-powered torches and most of us use low-energy light bulbs in our rooms at home.
We all come to school by car. None of us would cycle because it's too dangerous and ...

Reading

5 Read about some energy-efficient schools around the world.
Does your school have any of the same features?

Our school in Bali is made entirely from bamboo. It has clean energy systems like solar power, a biomass boiler and a micro-hydro generator.

Our school in Iceland and all our homes are heated by geothermal power. There are more than 200 volcanoes in Iceland and 600 hot springs which provide geothermal energy. We also have hydroelectric power from rivers and waterfalls. In fact, Iceland is the world's largest green energy producer.

Our school in Britain is heated by IHT – that's 'Inter-seasonal Heat Transfer'. There is a network of water pipes under the playground. When the sun shines, the playground heats up. This heats the water in the pipes, which is stored in insulated thermal tanks under the school. The stored heat is released into the school during cold weather. By using the same technology, the cold from winter can be stored to cool the building in summer.

Writing

6 Which of the energy-efficient features in Exercise 5 would be practical in your school? Which would not? Give reasons for your answers.

The power of nature

- Imagine a day without electricity. What would it be like?

Reading

1 Read the descriptions of various sources of energy. Which are renewable and which are non-renewable?

2 Work in pairs. Ask and answer these questions.

1 What is a wind turbine?
2 What are radioactive substances?
3 What is the difference between fossil fuels and nuclear fuels?
4 Can you only produce geothermal energy in volcanic areas? Give reasons for your answers.
5 Which of the energy sources described would be most suitable for future energy provision in your country and why?

Use of English: Future continuous

Use the future continuous to talk about what will be happening at a particular time in the future.

will   be   verb + -ing

As the century goes on, more and more people will be using renewable energy.

The blades on a wind turbine are moved by the **wind**. This creates energy that drives a generator.

In volcanic areas, the radioactive substances, such as uranium, in the rock release **geothermal** energy underground. This forces water and steam to the surface, which is used to drive generators. In non-volcanic areas, where there are hot rocks underground but no water, a pump forces cold water into the ground. It then rises as hot water and steam.

Water can be used to generate energy in several ways. The movement of waves in the sea, a fast-flowing river, water coming down a waterfall and water released from a dam can all generate power.

Coal, oil and natural gas are **fossil fuels**. They are burned to produce electricity.

3 Write sentences using the verbs in brackets in the future continuous.

1 By 2030 most people in cities (*drive*) electric cars.

2 Water, wind and the sun (*produce*) most of the power we need by the middle of the century.

3 Very soon, countries like Sweden and Costa Rica (*generate*) all their electricity from renewable sources.

4 Countries that have a lot of sunlight (*export*) solar energy to countries which have less sunlight.

5 In 50 years' time, people (*not / use*) fossil fuels to provide electricity.

6 What's your opinion? (*everyone / use*) only renewable energy by the end of the century?

Speaking

4 Work in groups. Discuss the advantages and disadvantages of the types of energy generation you've just read about. Use these words to help you.

Adjectives

clean / dirty
safe / dangerous
cheap / expensive
reliable / unreliable
renewable /
non-renewable

Nouns

environment
global warming
climate change

Verbs

pollute
provide
generate

Solar energy is produced either by solar cells or solar panels. Solar cells (photovoltaic cells) convert sunlight into electrical energy. Solar panels don't generate electricity; they heat water that is pumped through them.

Project: Write a short report

5 Work in pairs. Write a report about energy generation.

Part one: The present

- Find out which sources of energy are used to provide power in your country. Use the information to produce a pie chart like this:

The main **nuclear fuels** are uranium and plutonium. They are not burnt to release energy. They produce energy through a chemical reaction in a nuclear reactor.

As the century goes on, more and more people will be using renewable energy.

The hope is that by 2050, we will be getting a third of our energy from renewable sources.

Wind

Oil
Coal
Gas

Biofuel 0.16%
Biomass 1.7%
Wind 2.3%
Solar 0.15%
Hydro 0.59%
Nuclear 7.8%
Coal 19.2%
Gas 34.6%
Oil 33.6%

Source: BP

Part two: The future

- Find out and write about your country's targets for renewable energy.
  The plan is that by 2020, we will be using more energy from solar and wind sources.

Industrial revolution

- **Topics** The importance of water in farming; the start of the Industrial Revolution in Britain; developments in food technology

- **Use of English** The passive (*It is thought that*, *It is thought to be*); past perfect continuous; relative pronouns

Water for food

- Why is water essential for life?

Reading

1 Read the text. Find the words *irrigate, irrigating* and *irrigated*. What is irrigation?

Water and agriculture

From earliest times, farmers have had to find ways of irrigating their land in order to grow crops. It is believed that Chinese engineers in the 5th and 6th centuries BCE were the first to develop ways of taking water to places where crops were grown.

However, it is thought that an Egyptian waterwheel was already in use as early as the 7th century BCE. Waterwheels moved water from low ground to high ground, to irrigate crops. This meant that even land that was not near water could be used for growing crops.

In mountainous areas around the world, terraces were built to make good use of shallow soil and to create areas that could be irrigated for growing food. The Incas, for example, built terraces on the slopes of the Andes, where they grew crops such as potatoes. Canals, just a metre wide, were constructed to bring water from higher in the mountains to each terrace level.

Farmers in areas with little or no rainfall are now growing crops without soil. The system is called hydroponics. Plants are grown in a mineral solution that is pumped around their roots. The main advantage is that far less water is needed than for irrigating crops grown in soil because the water doesn't escape into the ground. Also, the water can be recycled. Other benefits are that the plants grow more quickly than in soil so that you get more food from the same amount of land.

Vegetables and salad are already grown hydroponically on the International Space Station. Plants grown hydroponically are considered to be a useful source of sustainable food for space missions.

2 Answer these questions. Give reasons for your answers.

1 Was the waterwheel a good idea?
2 Why do you think terraces were adopted by farmers in many countries around the world?
3 Is hydroponics a good idea? Will it be important in the future?

Use of English: The passive

The passive is useful in phrases such as:

It is / was believed that
It is / was thought that
It is / was said that

It means you don't have to specify exactly who believed, who thought or who said something.

Note that you can use an infinitive after a passive:

Plants grown hydroponically are considered to be a useful source of sustainable food for space missions.

---

3 Rewrite these sentences replacing the words in italics with a passive structure starting with *It*.

1 *People think that* wheat was first grown in Mesopotamia.
   It is thought that wheat was first grown in Mesopotamia.
2 *We know that* the Incas grew about 2000 different types of potatoes.
3 *People think that* the Incas were not the first to use irrigation canals in South America.
4 *We know that* the Romans grew grapes in Britain.
5 *Some people say that* you should drink two litres of water a day.

4 Rewrite these sentences replacing the words in italics with a passive structure followed by an infinitive.

1 *People think this waterwheel is over 2000 years old.*
   This waterwheel is thought to be over 2000 years old.
2 *People believe that hydroponic methods are* the future for farming in dry areas.
3 *People think that some olive trees are* over a thousand years old.
4 *Farmers considered that terracing was* the answer to growing crops in mountainous areas.
5 *Everyone says that water is* the most precious of all our resources.

Speaking

5 Work in groups. What do you know about agriculture in your country, present and past? Discuss the following questions.

1 What kind of crops are grown in your region? Are they the same now as in the past?
2 What kind of animals are raised on farms in your area?
3 How have farming methods changed?
4 Is agriculture more important or less important than it was in the past?
5 How is land irrigated in your country? Where does the water come from?

Writing

6 Write a paragraph about agriculture in your region for a web-based guide to your country. Include some of the phrases from the Use of English box.

In the past, terraces were used to grow … . You can still see …
It is thought that irrigation was introduced by …
It is believed that horses were brought to this country by …
This region was considered to be one of the most fertile areas in …

Full steam ahead!

- The Industrial Revolution was a period of great change in Britain, when manufacture by machines took the place of handmade goods. How do you think this changed people's lives?

Reading

1 Read the text at the bottom of these two pages about the Industrial Revolution in Britain. Which two aspects does it focus on?

2 Answer these questions.

1 What was the difference between Newcomen's and Watt's steam engines?

2 How did Arkwright change the way people worked?

3 Why do you think Arkwright built cottages for his workers?

4 What might the problem be in relying on water power? How did Arkwright solve this problem?

5 In your opinion, whose was the most important invention: Newcomen's, Watt's or Arkwright's?

6 Steam power went on to have many uses in the 19th century. Can you think of any?

Use of English: Past perfect continuous

Use the past perfect continuous to talk about actions or situations that had continued up to a time in the past.

Up to then, people had been working in their homes, spinning cotton by hand.

Arkwright had been using water power in his mills before he began to use a steam engine.

You can use the past perfect continuous to describe the cause of an action or a situation in the past.

He'd been working in the factory all day, so he was tired and hungry.

1712

In 1712, Thomas Newcomen invented a steam engine that could be used to pump water out of deep coal mines.

1769

Then in 1769, James Watt improved Newcomen's engine by adding a condenser which prevented the steam from escaping and was therefore much more efficient. Newcomen's and Watt's steam engines are considered to be the foundation of the industrial revolution. For several years, the machines continued to be used to pump water out of mines, but it was gradually understood that they could have other uses. One of these uses was in the cotton mills.

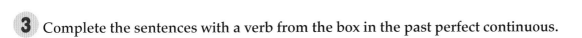

3 Complete the sentences with a verb from the box in the past perfect continuous.

do	not go	live	rain	spin	work

1 The river was very high because it _had been raining_ continuously for three weeks.
2 They _____ in a small village before they moved to the city.
3 Before she went to work in the factory, she _____ cotton at home.
4 The boy's clothes were black because he _____ down the mine.
5 Until a law called the Factory Act was introduced in 1833, children _____ dangerous work in the factories.
6 The boy couldn't read or write because he _____ to school.

Listening 13

4 Listen. Which aspect of the Industrial Revolution is the focus of this programme?

1 the different kinds of machines used in the mills
2 conditions for workers in the mills
3 people travelling long distances to find work

5 Listen again and complete this summary of what Professor Johnson says.

Children as young as 6 years old _worked in the mills._
They worked from …
Accidents were very common. For example, …
The factory workers suffered from chest and lung diseases because …
Factory owners preferred to employ …
Money was taken from their wages if they …

Speaking

6 Work in groups. Talk about what it must have been like to be a child working in a factory in Britain at the end of the 18th century.

Remember you can use the structure:
must have
might have   +   past participle
can't have

It must have been . . .

Writing

7 Write an account of a day in the life of a factory worker of your age in the 18th century. Use the information from Exercise 5 to help you.

We have to get up at 5.30 a.m. every day. …

1771

In 1771, Richard Arkwright set up a large water-powered mill to drive a cotton-spinning machine which was known as the Water Frame. Up to then, people had been working in their homes, spinning cotton by hand. But Arkwright brought the workers together in one place. He built cottages for them close to his mills. He welcomed large families so that women and young children could work in his factories.

1790

Arkwright had been using water power in his mills for almost 20 years before he began to use a steam engine to pump water to the waterwheel which drove the spinning machines. The steam engine ensured a continuous supply of power, making Arkwright's mills much more efficient and productive.

Can it or cool it!

- How many ways of preserving food can you think of?

Reading

1 Which two ways of preserving food are the subject of this article?

Food that is frozen, refrigerated or tinned, cans of drink … we take them for granted.

But before the Industrial Revolution, most people either grew their own food or had to buy it daily from markets. Factory workers and people who lived in cities didn't have time or space to grow their own food so new ways had to be found to feed them.

Tinned food has an interesting history. In the early 1800s, Napoleon Bonaparte offered 12,000 francs as a prize to anyone who could find a way of preserving food for the soldiers in his army. Nicolas Appert, a chef in Paris, won the prize when he showed that food could be kept in glass bottles that had been sealed and then boiled in water.

Then, in London, in 1810, Peter Durand made a cylindrical tin can which could be used to preserve food, using the same method as Nicolas Appert. Cans were lighter, unbreakable and easier to seal and transport. The cans were expensive because they were made by hand and they were difficult to open. However, by the end of the 19th century, production of airtight cans became mechanised. Tinned food was in great demand to feed the growing urban populations.

People had been using ice to preserve food for centuries but it wasn't until 1882 that the first refrigerated ship, the Dunedin, revolutionised the transportation of food. A steam-powered machine chilled the area where the food was stored, keeping it below freezing, which enabled the ship to successfully deliver a cargo of meat and butter from New Zealand to England. The ship set sail on 15 February 1882 and the voyage took 98 days. A few days after its arrival in London, *The Times* commented, 'Today we have to record such a triumph over physical difficulties as would have been incredible, even unimaginable, a very few years ago.'

The Dunedin

2 Find the names of the following in the text:

1 the leader of an army
2 an old kind of money
3 a French chef
4 a British inventor
5 a ship
6 a newspaper.

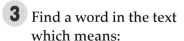

3 Find a word in the text which means:

1 closed so that nothing can get in or out

2 heated until bubbles and steam are produced

3 closed so that air cannot get in or out

4 done by machines

5 made cold (*two possibilities*)

6 the goods carried by a ship.

4 Answer these questions.

1 Providing food for their families was a problem for workers in the factories and the mills. Why?

2 Why did Nicolas Appert win 12,000 francs?

3 What were the first tin cans like?

4 What was important about the Dunedin's voyage in 1882?

5 How would you describe the attitude of *The Times* journalist to the Dunedin's voyage?

Speaking

5 Work in small groups. Discuss the following:

1 Why did Nicolas Appert need to seal and boil the bottles to preserve the food?

2 Why are cans useful for preserving food?

3 Why does keeping food cold or frozen preserve it? (*Think of bacteria …*)

Use of English: Relative pronouns

Remember to use *who* for people, *which / that* for things and *where* for places.

Factory workers and people *who* lived in cities didn't have time or space to grow their own food.

Food could be kept in glass bottles *that* had been sealed and then boiled.

Peter Durand made a cylindrical tin can *which* could be used to preserve food.

A steam-powered machine chilled the area *where* the food was stored.

6 Write definitions of the following using a relative pronoun in each one.

1 a refrigerator   *A refrigerator is a machine that keeps food cool.*

2 farm   *A farm is a place where crops are grown and animals are kept.*

3 chef

4 tin can

5 soldier

6 mill

7 steam engine

8 factory

Project: Industry in my country

7 Prepare a presentation for your class or another class on the history of industry in your country. Work in groups.

● To get you started, answer the following questions:

1 What were the main industries of the past? (When and where?)

2 Do they still exist? If not, why not?

3 What are the most important industries in your country at the moment? Where are they? When did they begin? Why are they important?

mining   forestry   fishing   textiles   oil / gas / coal   engineering   technology

● Divide the work among the members of the group. Decide who is going to research information, find illustrations, prepare the slides, etc.

● Plan your presentation and write a draft.

● When you've checked your work, present it to the class.

Memoir (14)

A Yorkshire Childhood   *c. 1842*
George Oldfield

Did you know?

The letter c before a date is short for *circa*, the Latin word for 'about'.

1 A memoir is a personal account by someone of people they have known or events they have experienced. What would you expect to find in a memoir of a child who worked in a factory in England in the 1840s?

2 Read the extract from George Oldfield's memoir written in about 1842. How does it make you feel?

3 Read the extract again and answer the questions.

1 What was the first bad thing that happened in George's life?
2 How old was he when he started working in a factory?
3 How many hours a day did he work?
4 Why did he curse the road that he and the other children walked on?
5 Did George's childhood experience have a lasting effect? How do you know?

4 Answer the questions about the way the memoir is written.

1 George creates a very clear picture of what life was like for a child factory worker. How does he do it?
2 In which sentences and phrases does he express his personal feelings?

5 Work in groups. Discuss the following:

How is a memoir like George's different from an account by a professional historian?

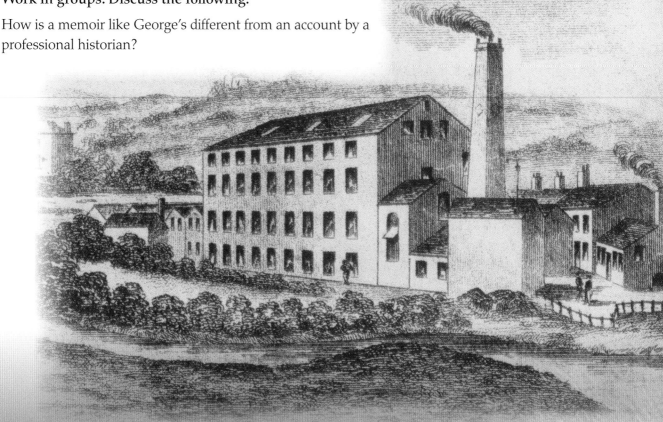

Rawford's Mill, near Huddersfield

A YORKSHIRE CHILDHOOD

My father's native place was Honley, about 7 miles from Huddersfield. His parents were poor working people – so much so that they had to get rid of their children as best they could; so my father was a town's apprentice to a farmer – he got his food but no wages at a village,
5 Crossland Hill, his master finding him what clothing he thought useful, while he was of age. After his apprenticeship he went to work in the stone quarries. In due time he got married, and there was a family of 3 children. I was the second, and had 2 sisters. Poor mother died when I was between 2 and 3. My eldest sister went to work in the factory
10 very early. I soon had to follow, I think about 9 years of age. What with hunger and hard usage I bitterly got it burned into me – I believe it will stay while life shall last. We had to be up at 5 in the morning to get to the factory, ready to begin work at 6, then work while 8, when we stopped half an hour for breakfast, then worked to 12 noon; for
15 dinner we had 1 hour, then work while 4. We then had half an hour for tea, and tea if anything was left, then commenced work again on to 8.30. If any time during the day had been lost, we had to work while 9 o'clock, and so on every night till it was all made up. Then we went to what was called home. Many times I have been asleep when I had
20 taken my last spoonful of porridge – not even washed, we were so overworked and underfed. I used to curse the road we walked on. I was so weak and feeble I used to think it was the road would not let me go along with the others.

by George Oldfield

get rid of *(line 3)* take action so that something or someone is no longer with you

apprentice *(line 4)* someone who has agreed to work for a skilled person for a period of time in order to learn that person's skills

wages *(line 4)* a fixed amount of money that is paid for work, usually every week

while he was of age *(line 6)* in Yorkshire, people use 'while' to mean 'until', as well as 'during the time'. This phrase means: 'until he was no longer a child, until he was old enough to earn money by working'

quarries *(line 7)* places where stone is dug out of the ground, usually for building

while 8 *(line 13)* until 8

half an hour for tea *(line 15)* a break of half an hour at 'tea time'

... and tea if anything was left *(line 16)* and something to eat if there was anything left

till it was all made up *(line 18)* until we had done all the work we had missed

curse *(line 21)* say bad things about

feeble *(line 22)* with very little strength

Review of Units 7–8

Vocabulary

Energy and the environment

1 Write the opposite of each adjective.

1 clean   d_____
2 safe   d_____
3 cheap   ex_____
4 dark   l_____

2 Use the correct prefix to make the opposite of these words.

> in   un   non-

1 reliable   _____
2 renewable   _____
3 active   _____

3 Make compound adjectives from the words in the two columns.

1b eco-friendly

1 eco-   **a** neutral
2 solar-   **b** friendly
3 longer-   **c** powered
4 energy-   **d** thermal
5 geo   **e** electric
6 hydro   **f** lasting
7 carbon-   **g** efficient

4 Use four of the adjectives from Exercise 3 to complete the following sentences.

1 Take a _____ phone charger with you because you might not be near any sources of electricity.
2 Swim in Iceland's hot water springs, heated by _____ power from deep underground.
3 Take a test drive in one of our new _____ cars which use much less fuel.
4 Enjoy Sweden's wonderful scenery, including its many rivers which are valuable sources of _____ power.

5 Make the nouns from these verbs. Note: they all end in *-tion*.

1 pollute
2 generate
3 irrigate
4 react
5 invent
6 produce

6 Complete these sentences using the words in the box.

> fossil   nuclear   photovoltaic
> reaction   turbine   warming

1 A wind _____ is a machine that uses wind to create energy.
2 Oil, coal and natural gas are _____ fuels.
3 Uranium and plutonium are _____ fuels.
4 The gradual increase in the Earth's temperature is called global _____ .
5 Another term for 'solar cells' is '_____ cells'.
6 When chemicals combine and form new substances, we call it a chemical _____ .

7 Write the words for the definitions.

1 flat areas of land built like steps on a mountain side and used for growing crops
2 man-made water channels or waterways
3 the science of farming
4 a method of growing plants in a solution of water and minerals, without soil
5 a hole or system of holes underground from which coal and other minerals are taken
6 a factory where a substance such as paper, cotton or flour is produced

Use of English

8 Add the missing word to these sentences.

1 Some of children who worked in the mill were as young as 6.
2 Each the families lived in a small cottage close to the mill.
3 It was such hard life for the mill workers.
4 Neither Jim's parents could read or write.
5 Most of older workers developed chest and lung diseases.

9 Use the prompts to write sentences about life in the future. Follow the model.

1 Robots / do / most of the jobs in the home. *Robots will be doing most of the jobs in the home.*
2 More people / work from home.
3 Children / learn from the Internet. They / not go / to school.
4 Factories / not use fossil fuels.
5 people / live / on Mars / ?

10 Use the prompts to write sentences showing what had been happening in each of the following situations.

1 When I got home there was a lovely smell in the kitchen.
Somebody / make / bread.
Somebody had been making bread.
2 I was in a strange place and I felt absolutely terrified. Then I woke up.
I / dream.
3 I wondered why I hadn't had a reply.
I / use / the wrong email address.
4 They couldn't find the key to the house.
They / not look / in the right place.
5 He fell asleep while he was eating his supper.
He / work / so hard all day.

General knowledge quiz

11 Work in pairs. Ask and answer the questions.

1 What is the population of Costa Rica: 4.8 million, 8.4 million or 48 million?
2 What colour is associated with being eco-friendly?
3 What does a biomass generator do?
4 Name three kinds of fossil fuels.
5 Name two kinds of nuclear fuels.
6 What did the Ancient Egyptians and the Chinese use to move water from low ground to high ground?
7 What did Thomas Newcomen invent in 1712 and what was it used for?

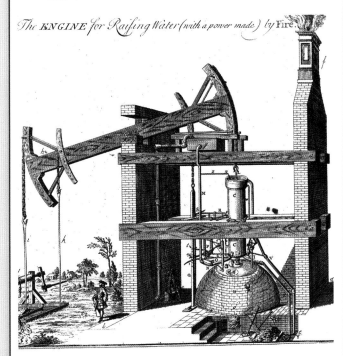

The ENGINE for Raifing Water (with a power made) by Fire.

8 Why did the Parisian chef, Nicolas Appert, win a prize offered by Napoleon Bonaparte?
9 What was the Dunedin and how did it revolutionise the transportation of food?
10 Look at the picture. What is it and why is it important in the history of food?

- **Topics** Statistics; reporting facts; collecting data
- **Use of English** Comparatives and superlatives (*more, most, less, least, fewer, the fewest*); complex noun phrases

Facts and figures

- In which school subjects do you have to handle data (in other words, work with facts and figures)? Give examples.

Reading

1 Read the information in the chart and choose the correct option.

The chart shows the relative number of people who:

a attended certain Olympic events

b looked up information about them online.

Popularity of sports at the Olympics

Sport	%
swimming	10.1%
gymnastics	7.6%
athletics	7.2%
football	4.2%
volleyball	4.1%
basketball	3.8%
cycling	3.4%
badminton	2.2%
sailing	1.9%
boxing	1.0%

0%   4%   8%   12%

The information in the bar chart shows the web page views for certain sports as a percentage of the total number of page views to the official Olympics website.

Language tip

Remember that with short adjectives you add *–(e)r* to make the comparative and *–(e)st* to make the superlative:

faster, fastest   NOT   ~~more fast, most fast~~

But note that you say *less fast, the least fast*.

Use of English: Structures using comparatives and superlatives

Comparative	Superlative
more	most
less	least
fewer	fewest

You can use *more* and *(the) most, less* and *(the) least*:

- **before adjectives**: *more / less / the least popular*
- **before nouns**: *more / less / the least interest*

BUT

Use *few* and *the fewest* with plural nouns: *fewer spectators / the fewest spectators*

- **before adverbs**: *more / less / the least quickly*

2 Read the Use of English box. Then complete these sentences, using the information in the bar chart in Exercise 1 and *more, most, less, least, fewer, fewest*.

1 Cycling was _____ popular than badminton.

2 Swimming was _____ popular sport.

3 Basketball was _____ popular than volleyball.

4 The _____ popular sport was boxing. It had the _____ page views.

5 _____ people were interested in badminton than in cycling.

6 Athletics was slightly _____ popular than gymnastics.

3 Record the following information in a two-column table.

Number of students	Percentages
2	21%–40%

In a class of 30 students, two students got between 21% and 40% in their Science test, eight scored between 41% and 60%, 16 students got between 61% and 80% and four students got between 81% and 100%.

4 Now represent the data from the table in a bar chart and a frequency polygon.

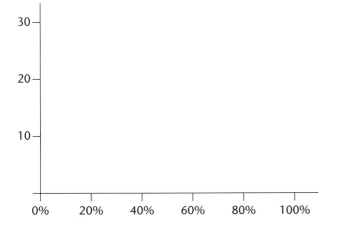

Language tip

You can use pronouns such as *everyone* and *no-one* to talk about numbers of people.

And you can qualify them with words like *almost* or *hardly*:

almost no-one

hardly anyone

almost everyone

5 Complete these sentences to describe the information shown in your bar chart / frequency polygon.

1 No-one

2 Hardly anyone

3 Almost everyone

4 A few

Speaking

6 Now use the results of a test that your class has done recently in English, or another subject, to produce a bar chart / frequency polygon like the one in Exercise 4.

- Start by finding out the results.

Put your hand up if you got between zero and twenty per cent.

- Record the results in a tally table like this:

Percentage	Tally	Frequency
0–20		
21–40	IIII III	8
41–60		
61–80		
81–100		

7 Discuss your results. Is your bar chart / frequency polygon similar to the one in Exercise 4?

What are the facts?

● 'The fewer the facts, the stronger the opinion.' What do you think this means?

Reading

1 Read these three newspaper articles. What do they have in common?

A

More than 90% of British teenagers have a mobile phone, which they usually take to school. Schools, however, are rethinking their mobile phone policy because a recent study by the London School of Economics has shown that banning them in school improves students' results.

Researchers looked at schools in four English cities and found that exam marks went up by more than 6% after banning phones.

B

According to a recent study, banning mobile phones from schools significantly improves results. Almost all British teenagers own a mobile phone and the study has shown that banning the phones reduces inequality between high-achieving and low-achieving students.

The research took a sample of schools in four English cities and found exam results improved by over 6% after banning phones, with low-achieving students and those from low-income families improving the most.

Strict mobile phone policies had little effect on both high-achieving students and younger teenagers. It is thought that high achievers are less likely to be distracted by mobile phones and that younger teenagers use phones less often.

However, there is at least one argument against banning mobiles. A complete ban prevents students from getting in touch with their parents when they might need to.

C

A recently published survey has caused schools to rethink their policy on mobile phones. Richard Murphy and Louis-Philippe Beland surveyed 91 schools in four English cities (Birmingham, London, Leicester and Manchester) before and after mobile phones were banned in the classroom. Mobile phone ownership among British teenagers is high, at 90.3%.

The 12-year study found that students' exam results improved by 6.4%. Low-achieving students benefited most from the ban, with test scores increasing by 14.23%. The study concluded that banning phones for these students was equivalent to an additional hour a week in school, or to increasing the school year by five days.

2 Copy the chart into your notebook. Read the texts again and complete the chart.

	Text A	Text B	Text C
Number of teenagers who have mobiles	90%	Almost all	
Number of cities in survey	4		
Which cities?			
Number of schools in survey			
Number of years covered by survey			
Percentage improvement in exam results			
Who benefited most?			
Who benefited least?			
Effect of mobile ban on time spent studying			
Any disadvantages of ban?			

Speaking

3 Work in groups. Discuss these questions. Give reasons for your answers.

1 Which of the articles gives the most specific data?

2 Which of the articles gives the most arguments for and against the banning of mobile phones?

3 Why do you think banning mobile phones in schools is the equivalent to adding an hour into the school timetable every week?

Use of English: Complex noun phrases

Complex noun phrases are common in English.

● noun + noun:
exam results

● adjective + noun + noun:
mobile phone policy

● compound adjective + noun:
high-achieving students.

4 Find in the articles the complex noun phrases which mean the following:

1 students who achieve high marks for their work and in exams

2 families whose income is low

3 a survey which has recently been published

4 ownership of mobile phones

5 a study which lasted 12 years

6 the time you spend at school during a year.

Speaking

5 Work in groups. Discuss reasons for and against banning mobile phones in schools.

Writing

6 Write an article for a newspaper giving the arguments for and against banning mobile phones in school. Make sure you support your arguments with examples and evidence where possible.

● Paragraph 1: Introduce the topic.
There has been a lot of discussion recently about whether mobile phones should be banned in schools. There is evidence to suggest that there should be a ban but there are also reasons for allowing students to have access to mobile phones.

● Paragraph 2: Give reasons for banning mobile phones.

● Paragraph 3: Give reasons against banning mobile phones.

● Paragraph 4: Draw a conclusion.

What can numbers tell you?

- If you had to promote and sell a new product, such as a smartwatch for teenagers, how might statistics be useful? Can you think of other kinds of work in which statistics are useful?

Reading

1 Read this extract from a book called *Statistics for Beginners*. Write the missing numbers in the spaces.

> When you have a set of numbers, you might want to find out the average. There are three different kinds of average: *mode*, *median* and *mean*.
>
> **1** The **mode** is the number that appears the most.
>
> 2 3 3 4 5 5 7 7 7 8 8
>
> In this set of numbers, the mode is ___ .
>
> **2** The **median** is the middle number.
>
> 2 3 3 4 5 5 7 7 7 8 8
>
> In this set of numbers the median is ___ .
>
> **3** If there are two numbers in the middle, the median is half way between them.
>
> 2 3 3 4 5 5 6 7 7 7 8 8
>
> In this set of numbers the median is ___ .
>
> **4** The **mean** is the total of the numbers divided by how many numbers there are.
>
> $3 + 6 + 7 + 8 + 8 + 8 + 9 = 49$
>
> In this set of numbers, the mean is ___ .
>
> **5** You may also want to find out the **range**, that is the difference between the biggest and the smallest number. To find it, subtract the smallest number from the biggest number.
>
> 2 3 3 4 5 5 7 7 7 8 8
>
> In this set of numbers, the range is ___ .

Listening 15

2 Listen to two students talking about the results of a history test. What are they calculating? Fill in the missing words.

History results	
1 _____ :	7
2 _____ :	6
3 _____ :	6
4 _____ :	5

Speaking

3 Work in pairs. Read the following and answer the questions.

You want to find out about how much you're going to have to pay for a new smartwatch. Four of the bestselling watches are listed on a website. The cheapest is $200, there's one at $250, one at $290 and there's another at $1000.

1 What is the range of costs?

2 What is the mean cost?

3 What is the median cost?

4 Which is more useful as a guide, the median or the mean?

Project: Design and write a questionnaire

4 Work in small groups. Your task is to design and write a questionnaire in order to produce a profile of a typical student in your class.

1 Before you write the questions for your survey, read the following guidelines.

- It's easier to collect and record information from structured questions rather than open-ended questions. Structured questions have a limited number of answers.
- Use questions requiring a *yes* / *no* answer.
- When giving a list of options, e.g. school subjects, add 'Other' to the end of the list.
- Be careful with overlapping categories, e.g. time spent:

0–59 minutes
1hour–1 hour 59 minutes

is better than

0–1 hour
1 hour–2 hours

- Ask only one question at a time; for example, don't ask 'Do you like Geography and History?'
- Make sure questions are specific. Don't use *sometimes*, *often*, etc.
- Don't ask personal questions.
- Make sure your questions are objective; in other words, don't show your own opinion in the question. For example, the question 'Do you agree that Maths is boring?' is not objective, because it shows you think Maths is boring.
- Never ask people to put their names on a questionnaire.
- If more than one answer is possible, add an instruction such as: 'Please select all the options that apply.'

2 Now write the questions. For your profile, you want to find out the following information:

1 hours you sleep per night
2 breakfast (every day)
3 travel to school
4 favourite school subjects
5 time you spend doing homework each day
6 number of books you have read in the last month
7 time you spend listening to music
8 hours you spend on a computer
9 mobile phone usage – texting, calls, apps, Internet
10 sports you take part in.

3 Check your questions against the guidelines above.

Student A: This question says: 'Do you usually have breakfast every day?' That doesn't make sense. You can't have 'usually' and 'every day' together. Anyway, the guidelines say we shouldn't use words like 'usually' in questionnaires.

Student B: OK, let's just put: 'Do you have breakfast every day?'

4 Hand in your questionnaires for your teacher to check.
5 Answer your questionnaire.

- **Topics** Giving presentations and speeches; presentation software
- **Use of English** Prepositional and phrasal verbs; reported speech – statements; pre-verbal adverbs (*first of all, next, finally*)

Picture it!

- There's a saying, 'A picture is worth a thousand words'. What do you think it means? Do you think it's true?

Reading

1 Read the advice on using presentation software. Match the list of headings to the paragraphs.

a What's it about? Tell them in your first slide.   **b** Get it right.   **c** Be prepared.

d Don't be a show-off!   **e** Don't rely on technology.   **f** Less is more.   **g** Empty slides can be useful.

h Make it readable.   **i** Make it visual.   **j** Your speech is more important than your slides.

Ten practical PowerPoint tips

1 Illustrate what you're saying by showing photos, graphs and diagrams.

2 Start with the slide that has the title of your presentation. Should you use a picture for the title slide? It depends on the subject and on whether you can find an appropriate picture.

3 You can put text on a slide but don't use too much. You want your audience to focus on what is important, so don't use more than eight lines of text and don't have more than eight to ten words per line. In most cases four lines of text is about right. Don't use too many slides and don't put too much information on your charts or graphs.

4 Use high contrast colour schemes for your slides and decide on a font that is clear.

5 Use just one type of transition and one kind of animation but don't overdo it.

6 Make sure that you can deliver your presentation without using the software.

7 When there's nothing that you want to illustrate, use a blank slide so that the audience looks at you, not at the slide from the previous point you were making. Also use a blank slide at the end of your presentation.

8 The most important thing is that the visual presentation is there to support your speech, not the other way round. You want your audience to concentrate on what you are saying.

9 Make sure you rehearse your presentation before you give it. Run through the slides.

10 Check your spelling, punctuation and grammar.

Speaking

2 Work in small groups. Discuss these questions.

1 What is the reason for each piece of advice in Exercise 1?

2 What other suggestions can you add to the advice?

Use of English: Prepositional and phrasal verbs

Some verbs like *put* can be followed by a number of prepositions / adverbial particles; for example:

put text on a slide

put a poster up

put your pens down

put your phone in your bag

Other verbs can only be followed by a particular preposition before an object. In the text in Exercise 1, several verbs are followed by *on*.

You can put text on a slide.

Don't rely on technology.

It depends on the subject of your presentation.

Find three more examples.

3 Use the prompts to complete the sentences. Remember to use the appropriate form of the verb.

concentrate		the bus being on time
not decide		the colour yet
depend	on	my homework
focus		the weather
rely		life in a small village in Kenya

1 We're thinking of having a barbecue, but it _____ .

2 Can you turn the music down, please? I can't _____ .

3 It was a really interesting TV documentary. It _____ .

4 I want to repaint my room but I _____ .

5 The bus is cheaper than the train but you can't _____ .

Speaking

4 Work in pairs. What is wrong with each of these presentation slides?

1

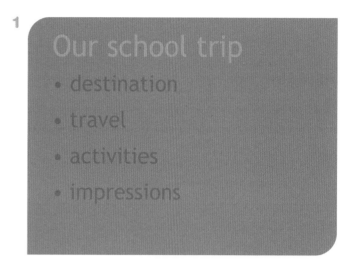

Our school trip
- destination
- travel
- activities
- impressions

2

In February our class went on a skiing trip to Italy.

We stayed at a youth hostel in Cervinia, close to the French border.

We had lessons every morning from 10 until 12 and then we had lunch.

After lunch, we went back to the slopes to practise.

By the end of the day, we were tired, but we were better skiers!

3

Getting your message across

- What might your teacher / headteacher say in an end-of-year speech?

  He / She might talk about the school trip.

  He / She would probably mention ...

  It's quite likely that he / she would talk about ...

Listening 16

1 Listen. Who is talking? Does she mention anything you thought of in answer to the earlier question?

2 Number the slides in the order in which the speaker in Exercise 1 uses them.

a   Music, drama and sport

b   Plans for a new drama studio

c   Academic achievement

d   Relations with the world outside school

3 Listen again. Then answer these questions.

1 What did the speaker say about the exam results?
She said that they were the best they'd ever had.

2 What did she say about the progress in Maths, English and Science?
She said ...

3 What did she say about the school play?

4 What did she say about swimming at the inter-schools sports event?

5 Why was she pleased that students had taken part in community events?

6 What did she say about plans for the future?

> **Use of English: Reported speech — statements**
>
> Remember that when we tell people what someone said, we usually change the tense because what they said was in the past.
>
> *'I'm not going to make a long speech.'* → *She said that she wasn't going to make a long speech.*
>
> *'I just want to say a few things about what we have all been doing over the last year.'* → *She said she just wanted to say a few things about what they had all been doing over the last year.*

4 It helps listeners to follow a talk if you tell them what you're going to say and do. Read the following list of useful phrases. Which ones are used in the speech you've just heard?

Introducing the topic	I'm going to talk about …
Giving an outline of what you're going to say	I'm going to divide this talk into four parts.
Starting	I'd like to begin / start by … First of all,
Moving on to a new section	Moving on now to … The next issue / topic / area I'd like to focus on … Next …
Giving examples	For example, … A good example of this is …
Summarising and concluding	And finally … To sum up … To conclude … In conclusion …
Inviting questions / comments	Does anyone have any questions or comments? Any questions?

Speaking

5 Discuss these questions.

1 Do you think the speech is well structured? Give reasons for your answer.

2 Do you think the slides were well chosen?

3 What effect do you think this speech would have on the listeners?

4 If you were choosing pictures to illustrate an end-of-year speech at your own school, what would you choose?

Writing

6 Write an end-of-term speech for your teacher / headteacher. Use your ideas from Exercise 5 and the useful phrases in Exercise 4.

I'm going to talk about …
I'd like to begin by …

From ideas into words

- When and why is it useful to work in groups?

Speaking

1 Work in small groups on the following task.

- Your teacher has asked you to come up with ideas for an English evening for parents. Two of you have suggested 'A profile of an English-speaking country' as the topic for the evening.

- You're going to talk about how to organise the evening and what to include. First, sort the phrases in the box into two categories:

Making suggestions and *Responding to suggestions.*

Have you thought of … ?	Perhaps you could …
I think you should …	That's a really good idea.
Yes, in fact we're thinking of …	Well, we could think about that but …
I'm not sure about that.	What about … ?
If I were you I'd …	What do you mean exactly?
It might be a good idea to …	Why don't you … ?
	You could …

- Share your ideas. Use the phrases above to help you.

> It might be a good idea to show a map of Australia.

- Decide how best to present each of your ideas. For example:
  - present an object such as a boomerang using 'show and tell' – in other words, show the audience the object and talk about it
  - a single image on a slide maybe enough to present, for example, the Sydney Opera House
  - give a PowerPoint presentation on the different regions of Australia.

Writing

2 Write a proposal to give to your teacher, giving details of your ideas for an English evening.

Proposal for an English evening

We would like to … because …

We're thinking of …

We could do a variety of things. For example, …

We believe that …

Language tip

Remember that prepositions such as *of* and *about* are followed by the *-ing* form.

We're thinking of giving a presentation about Australia.

What about including a short film?

Project: A presentation

3 You're going to prepare and give a five-minute presentation.

1 Choose one of the following topics or decide on your own topic.

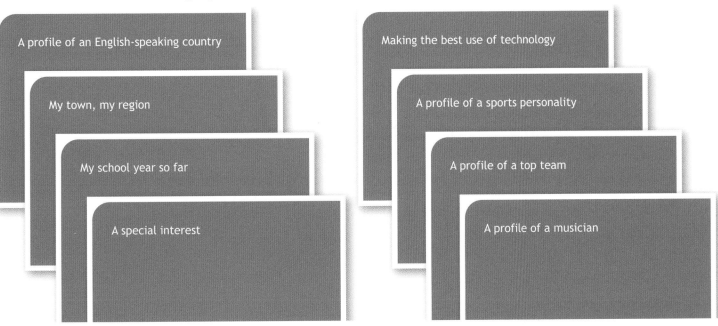

A profile of an English-speaking country

My town, my region

My school year so far

A special interest

Making the best use of technology

A profile of a sports personality

A profile of a top team

A profile of a musician

2 You're going to work individually on the topic you've chosen. But start by sharing your ideas in small groups. Use the words and phrases in Exercise 1 to help each other with ideas.

3 Working individually, write an outline of your presentation. Divide it into sections and think of at least one visual for each section.

4 Decide on the content of each section.

5 Use the useful phrases in Exercise 4 on page 81 to structure your presentation.

6 Write notes for your presentation.

7 Practise giving your presentation and time it. Remember your maximum time is 5 minutes.

8 Pick out the points to put on your presentation slides. Create your slides.

9 Rehearse your presentation with the slides.

10 Give your presentation.

Non-fiction 🔘17

A Little History of the World
E.H. Gombrich

1 Read about Ernst Gombrich and the extract from *A Little History of the World*. For whom do you think the book was written?

2 Read the extract again and answer the questions.

1 The writer refers to two important contributions to world knowledge from Arabic culture. What are they?

2 Look at the sentence 'The second is even more fabulous than the tales, although you may not think so.' Why do you think he adds the phrase 'although you may not think so'? (Remember who he was writing for.)

3 Which number system does the writer say is easier to work with, and why?

4 Which of the two contributions to world knowledge does the writer think has been more important?

3 Find examples of the following in the extract:

1 a topic sentence which introduces the topic of the paragraph

2 two sentences which refer to the things the writer likes

3 sentences making comparisons between two things

4 a sentence which refers back to the beginning of the paragraph and concludes it.

4 The writer uses the following techniques. Find examples of them in the text.

1 asking the reader questions

2 addressing the reader directly

3 using adjectives which show his opinion

4 making comparisons

5 humour

6 an informal conversational style

5 How would a reference book, e.g. an encyclopaedia or a school textbook, have treated this topic? How would it have been different?

6 Write a paragraph beginning:

There are two things for which I am especially grateful to my primary school teacher / my grandparents ...

Try to use some of the techniques used by Ernst Gombrich in the extract.

Ernst Gombrich wrote *A Little History of the World* in six weeks in the summer of 1935. It was translated into thirty languages but it wasn't until 2005 that his own translation into English appeared. He said *A Little History of the World* wasn't intended to be like a school history textbook: 'I would like my readers to relax, and to follow the story without having to take notes or to memorise names and dates'.

A LITTLE HISTORY OF THE WORLD

There are two things for which I am especially grateful to the Arabs. First, the wonderful tales they used to tell and then wrote down, which you can read in *One Thousand and One Nights*. The second is even more fabulous than the tales, although you may not think so. Listen! Here is a number: '12'. Now
5 why do you think we say 'twelve' rather than 'one-two' or 'one and two'? 'Because,' you say, 'the one isn't really a one at all, but a ten.' Do you know how the Romans wrote '12'? Like this: 'XII'. And 112? 'CXII'. And 1112? 'MCXII'. Just think of trying to multiply and add up with Roman numbers like these! Whereas with our 'Arabic' numbers it's easy. Not just because
10 they're attractive and easy to write, but because they contain something new: place value – the value given to a number on account of its position. A number placed on the left of two others has to be a hundred number. So we write one hundred with a one followed by two zeros.

Could you have come up with such a useful invention? I certainly
15 couldn't. We owe it to the Arabs, who themselves owe it to the Indians. And in my opinion that invention is even more amazing than all the Thousand and One Nights put together.

by E.H. Gombrich

Did you know?

There are seven symbols from which all Roman numbers are made:

I	1	C	100
V	5	D	500
X	10	M	1000
L	50		

There is no equivalent of 0.

Look at the numbers 1 to 12 on the clock face using Roman numerals. Explain how the Romans made the numbers 6, 7, 8, 11 and 12. Then explain how they made the numbers 4 and 9.

Review of Units 9–10

Vocabulary

Presenting information

1 Complete the newspaper report with the words below.

> low-achieving   improve   marks   per cent
> research   score   study   test

A _____¹ featuring 180 secondary schools students in Quebec, Canada, found that the _____² scores of students who had chosen a Music course were higher than those of students who hadn't chosen Music. Students who did Music got much higher _____³ in a range of subjects, including Science, Maths, History and Languages.

Another piece of _____⁴ has found that listening to music in Maths lessons can dramatically _____⁵ the results of _____⁶ students and help them to _____⁷ up to 40 _____⁸ higher in exams.

2 Complete the captions for these pictures.

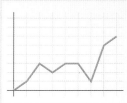

1 gr_____
2 di_____

3 ph_____
4 sl_____

5 ch_____

Use of English

3 Write the nouns from these verbs. They all end in *-tion*.

1 present   *presentation*   4 inform
2 animate   5 concentrate
3 illustrate   6 punctuate

4 Complete the phrases and sentences. Then copy the chart into your notebook and write the completed phrases and sentences in the chart.

a ___In___ conclusion …
b _____ example, …
c _____ sum up …
d A good example _____ this is …
e Does anyone have _____ questions?
f First _____ all,
g I'd like to start _____ showing you …
h Moving _____ now to …
i The next topic I'd like to focus _____ is …

Starting	1
	2
Moving on to a new section	3
	4
Giving examples	5
	6
Summarising and concluding	7
	8
Inviting questions / comments	9

5 Match the two parts of the sentences on the next page by referring to the chart of school subjects below.

Percentage of students taking these subjects:

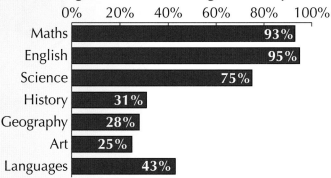

1 The most popular
2 Maths is slightly less popular
3 The least popular
4 Fewer students take
5 Art is slightly less popular
6 More students study
7 Art is the subject

a Science than Languages.
b with the fewest students.
c subject is English.
d Geography than History.
e than Geography.
f than English.
g subject is Art.

6 Use the following verbs with the correct preposition to complete the conversation.

put × 2	depend	rely	up
decide	concentrate		on × 4
			down

Anya: I want to _____¹ a mirror _____² on the wall but I can't _____³ _____⁴ the right place to put it. What do you think?

Rona: Well, it _____⁵ _____⁶ the size. Show me.

Anya: OK. I bought it at the market. I haven't had time to unwrap it. Oh, it's heavy. Let me _____⁷ it _____⁸ on the floor for a moment.

Rona: Actually it looks quite good there.

Anya: Do you think so?

Rona: The only problem is that if you put it there, you won't be able to _____⁹ _____¹⁰ your homework.

Anya: Why?

Rona: Because you'll be looking at yourself in the mirror all the time.

Anya: Ha, ha, very funny! I knew I could _____¹¹ _____¹² you to be helpful!

7 Report the following statements. Remember to change the tense of the verb.

1 Anya: It's heavy. *Anya said it was heavy.*
2 Anya: I bought it at the market.
3 Anya: I haven't had time to unwrap it.
4 Rona: It looks quite good there.
5 Rona: You'll be looking at yourself in the mirror all the time.

General knowledge quiz

8 Work in pairs. Ask and answer the questions.

1 What is the mathematical word for using information discovered from studying numbers?

2 What do you call information in an electronic form that can be stored and processed by a computer?

3 What is this called?

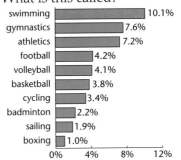

swimming	10.1%
gymnastics	7.6%
athletics	7.2%
football	4.2%
volleyball	4.1%
basketball	3.8%
cycling	3.4%
badminton	2.2%
sailing	1.9%
boxing	1.0%

0%   4%   8%   12%

4 What is this called?

5 What is this called?

Percentage	Tally	Frequency
0–20		
21–40	ⅢⅢ Ⅲ	8
41–60		
61–80		
81–100		

6 There are three different kinds of average. What are they?

7 According to the saying, what is worth a thousand words?

8 In this set of numbers, what does the number 8 represent in statistical terms? 1 2 2 4 5 7 7 9

9 What percentage of British teenagers have a mobile phone? Between 70% and 80%? Between 80% and 90%? Over 90%?

10 What are these and what links them?

11 Learning and training

- **Topics** Teaching and learning; practical skills training; school life
- **Use of English** Prepositional and phrasal verbs to do with learning; quantifiers with uncountable nouns (*a piece of advice*); present perfect simple and present perfect continuous

Good teachers, good learners

- In the age of the Internet, do we still need teachers? Give your reasons.

Speaking

1 Work in pairs. What kind of person does each of the following need to be? What skills and knowledge do they need to have? Make notes.

- army instructor
- driving instructor
- fitness instructor
- primary school teacher

- university lecturer
- tour guide
- careers counsellor

a good sense of humour

well-organised

able to motivate

a good communicator

a leader rather than a follower

a good role model

good at multi-tasking

Listening 18

2 Listen to four short presentations from a careers day at a school. Who is giving each of the presentations?

3 Look back to your notes in Exercise 1. Can you add anything to them for the four people you've just heard?

Use of English: Prepositional and phrasal verbs to do with learning

Prepositional and phrasal verbs have two or even three parts:
I'm not very good at looking up words in a dictionary.
I try to get away with doing as little as possible.

You can say:
I'm not very good at looking up words in a dictionary.
OR
I'm not very good at looking words up in a dictionary.

But if the object is a pronoun (for example, *them* rather than *words*), you must separate the two parts of the verb:
I'm not very good at looking them up in a dictionary.
NOT
I'm not very good at looking up them in a dictionary.

Reading

4 Work in pairs. Read the sentences and work out the meaning of the underlined phrases from the context. Use a dictionary if you need to.

School subjects

1 I find Maths really difficult and I can't always _keep up with_ the rest of the class, which means that I _fall behind_.

2 I'm quite good at Maths but I can't _do without_ a calculator.

3 History isn't my favourite subject. I try to _get away with_ doing as little as possible.

4 I like English but I'm not very good at _looking up_ words in a dictionary.

5 I like creative writing. I'm good at _making up_ stories.

In class

6 My teacher says that even when I don't know something, I can always _come up with_ an answer.

7 I like _joining in_ discussions but I don't like standing up in front of the whole class to speak.

8 If I don't know the meaning of a word, I try to _work it out_ from the context.

9 In discussions, I've often got ideas but I'm not very good at _putting_ them _across_.

10 I'm not good at exams because I write too much and then I _run out_ of time.

Outside class and homework

11 If I'm absent from school, I try to _catch up_ by asking my friend to lend me his / her notes.

12 If I run out of time to do something in a lesson, I _finish it off_ at home.

13 When I get home, I like to _go over_ what we've done in class so that I remember it.

14 I always try to _read through_ my written work before I _hand it in._

15 I sometimes _put things off_ to the last minute so I don't always manage to finish my homework on time.

5 Note down the numbers of the sentences in Exercise 4 which apply to you. Which of the sentences are true for both you and your partner?

6 Rewrite these sentences replacing the words in italics with a phrasal verb from Exercise 4.

1 I find Physics hard because I _work more slowly than_ most of the other students in my class.
   I find Physics hard because I can't keep up with most of the other students in my class.

2 I'm good at _inventing_ excuses for not doing my homework.

3 We sometimes sing English songs in class and I always try to _participate_.

4 I know what I want to say but I can't always _express it_ well.

5 I started painting my bedroom wall but I _didn't have enough_ paint, so I couldn't finish it.

6 I finally thought of a good ending for my story so that I could _complete it_.

7 We're going to have a vocabulary test tomorrow so I need to _study_ the words _carefully_ tonight.

8 We need to _give_ our project _to the teacher_ tomorrow.

9 The exam was _delayed_ until Friday.

Writing

7 Write a profile of yourself as a learner. Use the sentences in Exercise 4 to help you. Adapt them where necessary, e.g.:

I'm quite good at English but I can't do without a dictionary.

I'm good at exams because I've learnt to plan what I write so that I don't run out of time.

Language tip

Prepositional and phrasal verbs are an important feature of conversational language. Using them helps you to sound more natural.

Team spirit

● Which useful skills are not usually taught at school?

Reading

1 Read the information on page 91. Where would you find it?

2 Work in pairs. Read the information again. Look up any words you don't know in a dictionary.

Language tip

A collocation is a group of words which often occur together.

3 Match the words in the two columns to make collocations.
Check your answers by referring to the text.

1	overcome	a	an emergency
2	administer	b	a fear (of heights)
3	dress	c	first aid
4	deal with	d	into practice
5	put theory	e	team spirit
6	build	f	wounds

4 Work in pairs. Using the collocations in Exercise 3, make questions and answer them.

1 How can you (1) *overcome a fear of heights?*
2 When might you need to (2) ... ?
3 How do you (3) ... ?
4 Have you ever had to (4) ... ?
5 Can you think of an occasion when you have (5) ... ?
6 What kind of activities help to (6) ... ?

Reading and speaking

5 Answer the questions. (For questions 1–4, the answers are in the text. But for questions 5–8, you'll need to come up with your own ideas.)

1 Who is the information on page 91 aimed at?
2 What is abseiling?
3 How do you prepare for finding your way across unfamiliar territory?
4 What might you have to do to complete an obstacle course?
5 Why do you need to wear a harness when you're abseiling?
6 When might you need to build a shelter?
7 How would you make a splint?
8 Why do you need a compass to help you navigate, especially at night?

Use of English: Quantifiers with uncountable nouns

Advice and *equipment* are uncountable nouns. You can't talk about ~~an advice / some advices~~, ~~an equipment / some equipments~~.

But you can talk about *a piece of advice* and *items of equipment.*

I have to give you just one piece of advice.

There are various items of equipment you need.

6 Use *piece of* or *item of* with the following uncountable nouns to complete the sentences.

clothing   furniture   information   news

1 I found a useful _____ in the guidebook.
2 That's an unusual _____. Is it a stool or a small table?
3 There's an _____ on the website that might interest you.
4 A waterproof jacket is an important _____ to take on a camping trip.

Cadets are young people, like you, who usually meet once a week after school at their army unit or at weekends. You'll learn basic skills such as bush survival, first aid and navigation by day and by night.

Abseiling and rope activities

Overcome your fear of heights by taking part in abseiling. You'll wear a harness and a helmet and you'll lower yourself from a high point to the ground.

Camping and other training

You'll learn to put up a tent and build a shelter. You'll also learn to store and prepare food.

First aid

First aid is an important skill to learn. You will be able to administer first aid on water or in the bush. You will learn to dress wounds and to make splints and stretchers. You will learn how to deal with emergencies.

Navigation

Learn how to navigate using a map and a compass. Start with e-learning and classroom instruction. Then put the theory into practice during day and night expeditions.

Boat and water skills

Go canoeing, build a raft and learn important swimming and life-saving skills.

Physical training

Participate in team sports to build team spirit. Do cross-country running carrying equipment. Do an obstacle course where you wade through mud, climb over walls and crawl through pipes. You will get dirty!

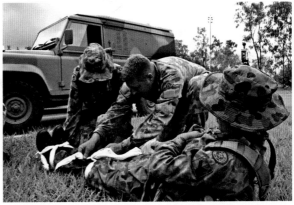

KW: I've just been on the cadet summer camp. It was really good fun. I recommend it but if I have to give you just one piece of advice it's this: take insect repellent. I didn't and I regret it!

SL: It's good mental and physical training. When you're going on a trek there are various items of equipment you need and you mustn't forget them.

What have you been doing?

● What have you enjoyed most this term?

Reading

1 Read the entries on the school website. Which school subjects are these students talking about?

2 Look at the three cartoons. Match each one to a text in Exercise 1.

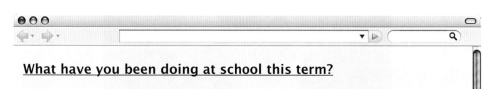

What have you been doing at school this term?

'We've had loads of homework this term and we've been learning our lines for the school play so we've been really busy.' *Amir*

'We've played in two inter–schools volleyball matches and we've won both of them, so our sports teacher is over the moon at the moment.' *Jade*

'We've written the words and music for a song. We're going to perform it this week.' *Alfie*

'I'm usually quite good with figures but we've been doing probability this term. I couldn't get my head round it to begin with but I'm beginning to get the hang of it now.' *Daniel*

'We've been working on an interesting project about ecosystems in South America. We've got to finish it off in the next couple of days because we've got to hand it in this week.' *Amelia*

'This term we've been learning about the Impressionist painters. We've had a go at doing an Impressionist picture ourselves.' *Lamin*

'We've been learning some poems by heart. I've really enjoyed it. There was one called "Let no one steal your dreams". It was the best ever!' *Fatima*

3 Find these idioms in Exercise 1. Then match them with their meanings.

1 loads of
2 to be over the moon
3 to get (my / your) head round
4 to get the hang of (something)
5 to have a go at (doing something)
6 to learn by heart
7 the best ever

a the most fantastic thing so far
b to be very happy
c to memorise
d to try to do something
e to understand (*2 phrases*)
f a lot of

4 Work in pairs. Make up a true sentence about your own experience using the idioms in Exercise 3.

I've had loads of homework this week.

I'm over the moon about ...

5 Read the Use of English box. Then choose the correct option in each of the following sentences.

1 What's the best book *you've ever read / you've ever been reading*?
2 How long *have you learned / have you been learning* English?
3 My clothes are wet because *it has rained / it has been raining*.
4 *We've had / We've been having* three tests this week.
5 *You've worked / You've been working* on your computer for too long. It's time to go to bed.
6 How long *have you known / have you been knowing* Ryan?
7 Why have you got mud all over you? What *have you done / have you been doing*?
8 I'm really sorry, but I *haven't had / haven't been having* time to finish off my project.

Project: Write a page for the school website

6 Write and design a page for the school website showing what the school has been doing this term.

1 Work in small groups. Brainstorm ideas for the content of the page. Think of:
- **Music and drama**
- **Sports events**
- **School clubs**
- **Other events**

2 Write the text and find a picture for each section.

Music and drama
Year 9 have been rehearsing for their production of *Treasure Island*, which will take place on ...

Sports events

School clubs

Other events

3 Decide on the best page layout for your material.
4 Read your text carefully. Check the punctuation and grammar.
5 Produce your web page.

Use of English: Present perfect simple and present perfect continuous

We use the **present perfect simple** to talk about past actions that are relevant now.

We've written the words and music for a song. We're going to perform it this week.

We use the **present perfect continuous** to talk about actions which started in the past and are still going on.

We've been learning our lines for the school play.

We also use the present perfect continuous for actions that have just happened and have visible results.

Why are you dressed as a pirate?

I've been rehearsing for Treasure Island. I'm the star!

Our school has taken part in several events this term, including the inter-schools games in which we won ...

12 Making a living

- **Topics** Jobs and aspects of work; part-time and summer jobs; young entrepreneurs

- **Use of English** Relative clauses with *which* referring to a whole clause; reflexive pronoun structures; present continuous passive

The ideal job

- What do you think is the best job in the world?

1 Read the results of a survey. Is there anything that surprises you?

Top 25 jobs according to 13- to 14-year-old British teenagers

1 actor / actress	10 singer / musician	18 manager (e.g. in an office / factory / shop / hotel)
2 lawyer	11 IT consultant	
3 police officer	12 graphic designer	19 hairdresser
4 doctor	13 fashion / shoe / jewellery / handbag designer	20 beauty therapist
5 sportsman / sportswoman		21 scientist
6 teacher / lecturer	14 dancer	22 mechanic
7 chef	15 vet	23 civil / mechanical / electrical engineer
8 accountant	16 TV or radio presenter / DJ	
9 member of the Armed Forces (soldier, etc), firefighter	17 artist	24 journalist
		25 airline pilot

From 'Education & Employers' (2010-2020) http://www.educationandemployers.org/research/taskforce-publications/

Speaking

2 Why do you think the top three jobs are actor, lawyer and police officer? What is attractive about these jobs?

3 Look at this list of the advantages of particular jobs. Six of the advantages are defined in the box. Which are they?

flexible hours

good prospects

good salary

interesting work

job satisfaction

long holidays

opportunities for travel

regular employment

seasonal work

serving the community

working outdoors

1   a lot of opportunities for future success

2   the enjoyment you get from doing your work

3   the time you start and finish work is not fixed

4   more than the average amount paid for the job you do

5   work that is only done at certain times of year

6   always having work

Listening 19 20

4 Listen to two teenagers discussing some of the jobs in the survey. Which six advantages from Exercise 3 do they mention?

5 You're going to hear an extract from a conversation about jobs. Answer these questions.

1 What job are they discussing?

2 What advantages are mentioned?

3 There's an inconsistency in what the boy says. What is it?

Use of English: Relative clauses with *which* referring to a whole clause

The pronoun *which* can refer to the whole of a previous clause.

| Clause 1 | Clause 2 |

People generally enjoy going to the theatre, which means that you get great job satisfaction from being an actor.

| Clause 1 | Clause 2 |

Working as a doctor involves helping people and serving the community, which I really want to do.

---

6 Join each pair of sentences together using *which*. Remember to use a comma before *which*.

1 Jobs that start and finish at the same time every day don't suit everybody. This is why jobs with flexible hours are becoming more popular.
   Jobs that start and finish at the same time every day don't suit everybody, which is why jobs with flexible hours are becoming more popular.

2 Being a police officer is challenging. This means that you have to be the right kind of person for the job.

3 My brother loves food and he loves cooking. That's why he wants to be a chef.

4 People usually feel better after a visit to the hairdresser. This makes you feel good about the job you do.

5 Being a firefighter means putting yourself in danger. I wouldn't like that.

6 If you are in the army or the navy, you get to travel a lot. This is something that I'd enjoy.

Speaking

7 Write a list of your own top ten jobs. Compare your list with others in the class. Is there one job which is the clear favourite of your class?

8 Work in pairs. Discuss the advantages and disadvantages of the first five jobs on your lists. Use the list of phrases in Exercise 3.

Writing

9 Write a paragraph explaining your first choice of job. Use the list of phrases in Exercise 3 and try to include some relative clauses with *which*, like the ones in Exercise 6.

To work in engineering you need to be good at solving problems, which I would enjoy ...

Part-time and summer jobs

- Would you like to have a part-time job? Why? / Why not?

Part-time and summer jobs

> **Am I allowed to get a job?**
> Babysitting
> Shop work
> Hairdressing
> Farmwork and gardening
> Working in a café
> Working at a riding stables
> Hotel work
> Office work

Am I allowed to get a job?

What the law in England says:

You have to be at least 13 to have a job.

If you're between 13 and 14, you can work for up to five hours a day on Saturdays and during school holidays. But you must not work for more than 25 hours a week.

All children must have at least two weeks when they're not working during the summer holidays.

Speaking

1 Work in pairs. Look at the website menu above. Ask and answer this question about each of the jobs.

What does (babysitting) involve?

2 Work in pairs. Read the section 'Am I allowed to get a job?' Ask and answer these questions.

1 Do you agree with the rules about jobs for teenagers? If not, how would you change them?

2 At what age can you get a part-time job in your country?

3 How many hours a week can a teenager in your country work?

3 Work in pairs. Read the list of questions about babysitting. Think of three more questions to ask.

> Am I allowed to get a job?
> **Babysitting**
> Shop work
> Hairdressing
> Farmwork and gardening
> Working in a café
> Working at a riding stables
> Hotel work
> Office work

Babysitting

What does the job involve?

How many children will I be looking after?

How long will I be expected to work?

Are the children allowed to help themselves to snacks and drinks?

Can I make myself a sandwich or a snack if I'm hungry?

Are the children allowed to use the computer by themselves?

Do the children put themselves to bed?

Where is the first-aid kit kept?

Are there any fire extinguishers? Where are they?

WORK

Use of English: Reflexive pronoun structures

We use reflexive pronouns when the subject and the object are the same.

subject   object

Are the children allowed to help themselves to snacks and drinks?

subject   object

Can I make myself a sandwich or a snack if I'm hungry?

The reflexive pronouns are:

singular	myself	yourself	himself / herself / itself
plural	ourselves	yourselves	themselves

4 Complete the sentences with the correct reflexive pronouns.

1 Is it OK if I help _____ to another piece of cake?

2 Does the oven switch _____ off when the timer stops?

3 Be careful, Sasha. You can hurt _____ if you carry boxes that are too heavy.

4 He had a great time working at the riding stables. He really enjoyed _____ .

5 Are we allowed to help _____ to snacks and drinks from the fridge?

6 She downloaded an app and taught _____ to play the guitar.

Speaking

5 Work in pairs. Look at the questions about babysitting in Exercise 3. Think of questions to ask about two of the other jobs in the list.

6 Work in pairs. Choose two of the jobs in the list and role-play conversations between the person thinking of taking the part-time job and the employer. Use your questions from Exercise 5.

Q What hours will I be expected to do?

A From 5 to 7 on Mondays and Wednesdays.

7 Work in groups. Read the newspaper extract and discuss this question: Is it a good idea for young teenagers to have part-time jobs?

Writing

8 Write a report of your discussion in Exercise 7.

Some people said that … . Others thought that …

'Around a quarter of all 13- to 16-year-olds in England take some formal paid employment during school term time. This can be a good thing. They earn their own money and can pick up useful skills, which might help them find full-time work in the future.'

However, Dr Holford's report went on to say that part-time work could have a negative impact on behaviour and exam grades.

Young entrepreneurs

● An entrepreneur is someone who has an idea for a business and makes it a reality.
What qualities do you think an entrepreneur needs to have?

Reading

1 Read the article. What do Conor Lynch and Anna Paris have in common?

Teenagers all over the world are being inspired by competitions such as *Junior Dragons' Den* and *TeenTech* to come up with their own inventions and products. They are being encouraged to become young entrepreneurs.

Dragons' Den is a TV programme that originated in Japan. The participants are entrepreneurs who want to get money and advice from successful businessmen and women to help them build their own businesses. Each participant is given three minutes to present their product.

Junior Dragons' Den is for young entrepreneurs between the ages of 12 and 18. Conor Lynch was one of the successful contestants.

Conor goes to school near Dublin in Ireland. He makes bowls, candle holders, clocks and other items from bits of wood. He won money to help him turn his hobby into a business.

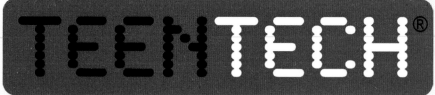

The *TeenTech* Awards encourage young people to develop their own ideas to make life better, simpler and easier with on-going support from experts across industry. The final is held at The Royal Society and the winners go to Buckingham Palace. The initiative has already seen products go to market and students retain their IP*.

Anna Paris and her team from Greenock in Scotland won a *TeenTech* award for her invention, the Chargicle. It's a charger that works with a bicycle. It charges your iPad, your tablet or your mobile phone while you're riding your bike. Anna's idea is being considered by technology companies who may want to manufacture it. Other *TeenTech* inventions were a touch-screen guitar teaching app, and a hi-tech frame to help disabled young people to take part in ice-skating.

* IP = intellectual property. This means that people are not allowed to copy what the students have invented.

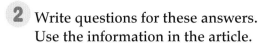

2 Write questions for these answers.
Use the information in the article.

1 They're competitions for young inventors and young entrepreneurs.
2 Japan.
3 Three minutes.
4 Between 12 and 18.
5 Bits of wood. (*Start your question with 'From'.*)
6 Her invention, the Chargicle. (*Start your question with 'For'.*)

Use of English: Present continuous passive

Remember that you use the present continuous for things that are happening now, at this moment, or for things happening around now.

Present continuous active
We are looking for the next generation of business people.

Present continuous passive
Teenagers all over the world are being inspired by competitions such as Junior Dragons' Den.

---

3 Use the present continuous passive to make the prompts in italics into full sentences.

1 There are lots of jobs in construction in the city at the moment. *A new shopping centre / build.*
   A new shopping centre is being built.
2 Sorry, you can't go in. *The candidates for Dragons' Den / interview.*
3 There's a special lunch for new employees today. *It / serve in the dining-room.*
4 You can do your on-line application later. *The computer / use at the moment.*
5 Come and look at this. *The TeenTech awards ceremony / show on TV.*
6 We're working on a really interesting project. *The problem is that we / not / give enough time to finish it off.*

Speaking

4 Discuss these questions.

1 Do you think competitions such as *Junior Dragons' Den* and *TeenTech* are a good idea? Give your reasons.
2 Are there any disadvantages of competitions like these?

Project: An application for a competition

5 Work in small groups. You're going to invent a product and write an application for a young entrepreneurs' competition.

1 Brainstorm ideas for a product to present at a young entrepreneurs' competition.
   Think of something that would be really useful to people of your age or that they would like to have. It can be an item of clothing, a fashion accessory, something you can eat or drink, a piece of equipment or a computer / mobile phone accessory.
2 Look at the questions on the application form. Discuss how you will answer them.
3 Complete the application by answering the questions in writing.
4 Check your answers for grammatical accuracy and punctuation.

The product
1 What is your product called?
2 Why would your product be useful?
3 What's special about it? What are its USPs (Unique Selling Points)?
4 Is there anything else like it on the market already? How is your product different?

Design features
5 What will your product look like? (Draw a picture or a diagram.)
6 What materials will you need to make it?

The costs
7 How much would the product cost to make?
8 How much would you sell it for?

Your market
9 What is your target market? Who is your product aimed at?
10 How will you advertise your product and where will you sell it?

Fiction ㉑

The Adventures of Tom Sawyer
Mark Twain

The Adventures of Tom Sawyer by Mark Twain was published in 1876. It's a novel about a young boy growing up by the Mississippi River. It's set in the fictional town of St Petersburg, which is based on Hannibal, Missouri, USA, where Mark Twain lived.

1 In the preface to *The Adventures of Tom Sawyer*, Mark Twain said that although he had written the book for boys and girls, he hoped that adults would read it too. Why do you think some children's books also appeal to adults?

2 Read the extract. Answer the questions.

1 What do you learn about Aunt Polly?
2 What do you learn about Tom?
3 Why does Tom think the other boys will make fun of him? *(line 33)*
4 What is Tom's 'brilliant idea'? *(line 34)*
5 What does Ben think when he sees Tom painting the fence?
6 Why doesn't Tom let Ben paint at first?
7 Why was this a good day for everybody in the end?
8 What is the lesson that Tom learns?

3 Look at the underlined phrases in these sentences from the extract. Can you think of another way of saying them?

1 The trouble is, he makes me laugh. *(line 22)*
2 The other boys will make fun of me. *(line 33)*
3 I bet you'd like to come. *(line 38)*
4 It's a shame you have to work. *(line 38)*
5 I can't believe my eyes. *(line 75)*

4 Answer these questions about the style of the extract.

1 What do you notice about the first nine lines of this extract from the story? What effect do they create?

2 Look at lines 27 to 29. Why does the writer begin this part of the story by describing the day?

3 Writers sometimes break grammatical rules. Look at the sentence in line 29: 'Everyone except Tom'. This is a sentence without a verb. What effect does it have?

5 Read what Mark Twain said about his book. Then work in small groups and discuss the questions below.

'Most of the adventures recorded in this book really occurred; one or two were experiences of my own, the rest those of boys who were schoolmates of mine. Huck Finn [another character who appears in *The Adventures of Tom Sawyer*] is drawn from life; Tom Sawyer also, but not from an individual – he is a combination of the characteristics of three boys whom I knew.'

1 What do you learn from the extract about the character of Tom? Why do you think he's become a well-known character in literature?

2 If you were a novelist, what would you write about and where would you get your characters from?

Norman Rockwell

THE ADVENTURES OF TOM SAWYER

"Tom!"
No answer.
"Tom!"
No answer.
5   "Tom, where are you!"
No answer.
The old lady went to the door and looked out into the garden.
"Tom!"
10   There was a noise behind her, and she turned around just in time to catch the jacket of a small boy who was trying to run past her.
"There you are! Why were you in the closet? What were you doing?"
15   "Nothing, Aunt."
"Nothing! What's that on your hands and your mouth? It's jam! You were eating my best jam!"
"Look behind you, Aunt!"
The old lady turned around quickly, and the boy
20   escaped. He climbed the garden fence and disappeared.
"I never learn," thought Aunt Polly. She smiled. "The trouble is, he makes me laugh. And he's my own dead sister's boy, poor thing. I can't be too strict with him. But he should learn. Tomorrow's Saturday, and when all the
25   other boys are having a holiday, Tom's going to paint the fence."

* * *

It was a perfect summer morning, warm and sunny. The birds were singing, and everyone in St Petersburg was happy. Everyone except Tom. He was standing by the
30   fence with a bucket of white paint and a paintbrush. The fence was thirty yards long and nine feet high. He started to paint. "It's going to be a long job," he thought, "and all the other boys will make fun of me."
Then he had an idea – a brilliant idea.
35   As Tom was painting, Ben Rogers came up the street. He was eating an apple.
"Hello, Tom," he said. "I'm going down to the river to go swimming. I bet you'd like to come. It's a shame you have to work."

40   Tom's mouth watered for the apple, but he continued to paint. He stood back from the fence to admire his work, like an artist.
"Work?" said Tom. "This isn't work. After all, you don't get the chance to paint a fence every day."
45   Ben watched as Tom was painting. He became more and more interested.
"Tom, let me paint for a time."
Tom thought about it. "No, I'm afraid I can't," he said. "Aunt Polly wants me to do it, because she knows I'll do it
50   so carefully."
"Just let me do a little bit," said Ben.
"Sorry," said Tom.
"I'll give you some of my apple."
"Sorry," Tom repeated.
55   "I'll give you *all* of my apple!"
"Well," said Tom after a pause, "all right. But make sure you do a really good job."
Tom sat down and ate the apple. As Ben was painting, Billy Fisher came by to laugh at Tom. But when he saw
60   Ben, he too wanted to try painting, and, in exchange for his kite, Tom let him. Then Johnny Miller came by. And in exchange for a toy soldier, Tom let him paint, too …
By the middle of the afternoon, the fence had three coats of paint on it, and Tom had a collection of all sorts
65   of things.
Tom said to himself that it wasn't such a bad world after all. If you make something difficult to get, people will always want it. He went into the house.
"Can I go and play now, Aunt?" he asked.
70   "What, already? How much have you done?"
"All of it."
"Don't lie to me, Tom."
"I'm not lying, Aunt Polly."
Aunt Polly went outside.
75   "Well, Tom!" she said. "I can't believe my eyes. Yes, you can go and play. And you can have the best apple in the bowl."

Adapted from The Adventures of Tom Sawyer *by Mark Twain*

closet *(line 13)* American English for a cupboard built into the wall of a room

yard *(line 31)* a unit of measurement (1 yard = 0.9144 metres)

feet *(singular foot) (line 31)* a unit of measurement. There are three feet in one yard (1 foot = 0.3048 yards)

Review of Units 11–12

Vocabulary

Jobs and professions

1 Match the words in the two columns.

1	driving	a	counsellor
2	university	b	guide
3	tour	c	instructor
4	primary school	d	lecturer
5	careers	e	teacher

2 Read the definitions and write the jobs.

Someone who ...

1 plays a part on stage in a theatre
2 defends people in a court of law
3 cooks food in a restaurant
4 deals with information about the money earned and spent by a person or a company
5 flies a passenger plane for a company.

3 Write the missing word to complete each sentence.

1 I'd like to have a go _____ setting up my own business.

2 I'd like to be an actor and I am quite good at learning things _____ heart.

3 I've just got a part-time job working in a stables. I'm _____ the moon about it.

4 I've only had three guitar lessons but I'm beginning to get the hang _____ it.

5 Statistics is a difficult subject but I'm beginning to get my head _____ it.

Use of English

4 Complete the text with the correct words from the list. You will need some of them more than once.

across	off	through
behind	out	up
in	over	with

I had to have two weeks off school earlier this term. I was worried that I would fall _____[1] and then not be able to keep _____[2] with the rest of the class.

When I went back to school, I read _____[3] my friend's Science notes. They'd been doing a project on electricity and the teacher had given them a set of questions. I managed to work _____[4] the answers quite easily so I handed _____[5] my work to the Science teacher and I got 90%. I was really pleased.

The English teacher saw me after school and went _____[6] what I'd missed. They had been studying *haiku* and making _____[7] their own poems. I managed to come _____[8] with four *haiku* poems. I had to look _____[9] some words in the dictionary but my teacher was really pleased. She said I'd got the hang of writing haiku poems and that I was good at putting my ideas _____[10].

Maths wasn't so easy. My class had been studying probability. I put _____[11] doing the work the Maths teacher had set me. I tried to get away _____[12] just reading the textbook but the teacher wanted me to do the exercises. I left it to the last minute and I almost ran _____[13] of time. However, I managed to finish it _____[14] last weekend.

So I have finally caught _____[15]!

5 What has been happening? Use the prompts to write the sentences.

1 A: What have you been doing?
   B: I / do / a crossword.   *I've been doing a crossword.*

2 A: You look tired.
   B: We / play / football since three o'clock.

3 A: What's the matter?
   B: We / wait / for the bus for two hours.

4 A: Why doesn't Tom want anything to eat?
   B: He / eat / ice cream all afternoon.

5 A: Have you finished off your homework?
   B: Not yet. I / have / rest.

6 Use the prompts to write the sentences with reflexive pronouns.

1 She's really good at playing the guitar and she's never had a lesson. (*teach*) *She taught herself.*

2 He had a great time at the summer camp. (*enjoy*).

3 A: The cake was delicious. Could I have another piece?

B: Of course. (*help*)

4 A: Oh no. Did you fall off your bike?

B: Yes, but don't worry. (*not hurt*)

5 A: Have you had anything to eat yet? You must be hungry.

B: Don't worry, we (*make*) some sandwiches.

7 Use the pictures to answer these questions. Use the present continuous passive, as in the example.

1 Where are your shoes?

2 Why can't we go into that room?

They're being repaired.

3 Where's Shona?

4 Why haven't they moved into their new house yet?

General knowledge quiz

8 Work in pairs. Ask and answer the questions.

1 What are the words for the following professions:

a a doctor for animals?

b someone who writes for a newspaper?

c someone who is a member of an army?

2 What is the name of this activity? You wear a harness and a helmet and you lower yourself from a high point to the ground using a rope.

3 What are these?

a

b

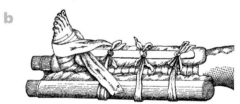

4 It means 'immediate help' and you might need it if you are wounded or injured. What is it?

5 What subject would you be learning if you were studying the Impressionists?

6 In England, how old do you have to be to have a part-time job: 11, 13 or 16?

7 In which country is Dublin?

8 What are *Junior Dragons' Den* and *TeenTech*?

9 Where did the TV programme *Dragons' Den* originate?

10 What is an 'entrepreneur'?

- **Topics** Population distribution and density; population pyramids; population and migration; vital resources – water
- **Use of English** Prepositions in the context of numbers and data; the future perfect; conjunctions

People and places

- In your country, where do most people live? Why do they live there?
  Are there any areas where very few people live? What's the reason for this?

Listening 22

1 Listen. What is the topic of this radio report?

2 Listen again and choose the correct answers.

1 Which two geographical areas of Brazil are mentioned?

a the north	c the south-east
b the south	d the north-east

2 Which three cities are mentioned?

a Recife	c Brasilia	e Manaus
b São Paulo	d Rio de Janeiro	

3 Brazil is the world-export leader in three of the following. Which are they?

a beef	c coffee	e orange juice
b cocoa	d sugar	

4 The city of Manaus was built using money from which of the following?

a coffee	b rubber	c wood

3 Explain the meaning of the phrases in italics. Listen again if you need to.

1 The major cities, São Paulo and Rio de Janeiro in the south-east, are *densely populated*.

2 There are *good communication links* with the rest of the world.

3 Outside the major cities, the south-east is *moderately populated*.

4 It is the most *sparsely populated* area of Brazil.

5 However, *there is one exception*.

Speaking

4 Work in groups. Discuss why the following geographical features affect where people live. You can refer to Brazil in your discussion.

- relief (mountainous areas, lowland areas, …)
- climate
- vegetation (forests, grassland, …)
- soil
- accessibility (roads, railways, ports, …)
- resources (water, wood, minerals, …)

Reading

5 Work in pairs. Look at the diagrams and read the explanation.
Does anything surprise you?

Brazil: population pyramids

In 1950, the largest sector of the population in Brazil was in the 0–5 age group. It represented approximately 8% of the total population. The number of people in each age group gradually decreased with age. This meant that the 'population pyramid' was a classic pyramid shape.

By 2000, this had changed. The percentage of people under the age of 5 was smaller than the percentage of people in the 15–25 age group. The 0–5 sector of the population had fallen to less than 5% of the total population, whereas the 15–25 age group had risen to more than 5% of the total population.

By 2050, it is estimated that the number of people between the ages of 0 and 30 will be only slightly smaller than the number of people in the 31–60 age group.

In the next two or three decades there will be a huge increase in the number of people in the 60–100 age group. It will have increased to 23.6% of the total population. The population pyramid looks more like a tower block with a small pyramid at the top.

6 Answer the questions.

1 What can you say about the number of people under the age of 5 in 1950 compared with 2000?

2 Compare the shape of the 1950 pyramid with the 2000 pyramid. What do you notice?

3 Now compare the population pyramids for 2000 and 2050. What do you notice about the under-5 age group?

4 What do you notice about the over-60 age group in the 2050 pyramid?

7 Complete the text using the correct prepositions.

below	between	from	in	of	to

Births and deaths are natural causes _____[1] population change. The difference _____[2] the birth rate and the death rate of a country is called the natural increase.
To work out the natural increase, subtract the death rate _____[3] the birth rate.
In some countries, the birth rate is declining. A recent study in Germany, for example, has shown that the country's birth rate has fallen _____[4] the lowest in the world.
In fact, in terms of the birth rate, Germany has now dropped _____[5] Japan.
However, globally the birth rate is far higher than the death rate. The increase _____[6] the population of the world is now 1 billion every 15 years.

> ## Use of English: Prepositions in the context of numbers and data
>
> Notice the prepositions used before these noun phrases:
>
> *in each age group*
> *under the age of 5 …*
> *between the ages of 0 and 30 …*
>
> Notice the prepositions used after these noun phrases and verbs:
>
> *an increase in*   *had risen to*
> *had fallen to*   *increased to*

Speaking

8 Work in groups. Discuss the possible reasons for changes in the shape of the population pyramids for Brazil in Exercise 5.

Japan: A case study

- A case study gives specific information about something in order to illustrate general principles. How might a case study in medicine or education, for example, be useful?

Reading

1 Read the article. What is the problem Japan faces?

Is immigration the answer for Japan?

Since the 1950s, the birth rate in Japan has been below replacement level. By 2050, the population will have fallen from today's 127 million to 95 million. What is more, by 2050 almost 40% of that 95 million will be over the age of 65, because life expectancy in Japan will have risen significantly.

"Population is a central problem confronting Japan. A falling birth rate and an aging population mean that the country has far too few young, productive workers. This will become even more noticeable as the current working generation begins to retire," says Hidenori Sakanaka, former director of the Tokyo Immigration Bureau. His solution is to welcome immigrant workers, some of whom would be care workers to look after the elderly. He estimates that Japan needs to accept about 10 million immigrants over the next 50 years.

"Because Japan has traditionally been such a homogeneous place," says Mr Sakanaka, "many have feared the prospect of greater immigration. Yet a pro-immigration policy doesn't have to undermine Japanese values or culture." It's a big step for Japan, but the country needs to become more multi-racial. At the moment, it's hard for immigrant workers to settle in Japan. They have to pass a very difficult Japanese language exam, and they are only allowed temporary residence. This needs to change.

Mr Sakanaka may not have all the answers, but he's making constructive and realistic proposals which should be considered.

2 Match the words and phrases from the text to their meaning.

1	confronting	a	consisting of people or things that are all of the same kind
2	care workers	b	old people
3	(the) elderly	c	facing (used in the context of difficult situations)
4	homogeneous	d	to make something weaker
5	prospect	e	the idea of something that will or might happen in the future
6	undermine	f	the right to live somewhere
7	multi-racial	g	people who are paid to look after other people
8	residence	h	formal suggestions
9	proposals	i	of many different races

3 Answer these questions.

1 'The birth rate in Japan has been below replacement level.' What does this mean?

2 What is 'life expectancy'?

3 What is a 'pro-immigration policy'?

4 Which of the following population pyramids represents the population of Japan in 2050, according to the article? Give reasons for your answer.

1

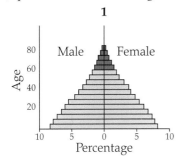

2

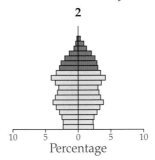

3

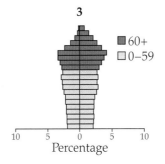

5 What are two of the problems faced by immigrant workers in Japan?

6 Can you tell what the writer's own opinion is? Explain your answer.

Use of English: The future perfect

We use the future perfect to say that something will have happened by a certain time in the future.

By 2050...   will   have   past participle

the population *will have fallen* from today's 127 million to 95 million.

The birth rate probably *won't have increased*.

Will we have started living on another planet?

---

4 Put the verbs in brackets in the future perfect.

1 By 2030, the population of the world (*increase*) by 1 billion.

2 By the time I leave this school, I (*be*) here for seven years.

3 By 2055, (*robots / take*) the role of care workers?

4 We have to hand in our project on Friday but we (*not / finish*) it by then.

5 When we see you next we (*do*) all our exams.

Speaking

5 Work in small groups. What will you have done by the year 2050?

6 Work in groups. Do you agree with any of these statements? Give your reasons.

1 I think it's the family's responsibility to look after the elderly.

2 I think it's the government's responsibility to look after the elderly.

3 When you get old, you should be in a special home for the elderly and you should be looked after by care workers.

Water for the world

● What are the implications of an increasing world population?

Reading

1 The following extract is from a magazine article about population growth. Why has the writer chosen to focus on water?

Experts are predicting that the global population will have reached between 8 and 11 billion by 2050 (it is currently 7 billion). This can only increase pressure on the planet's essential natural resources, such as oil, other fossil fuels and water. Either we start to think seriously about how to tackle the problem or we face a very uncertain future.

Water is our second most important resource for life, after air. Energy can be generated from renewable sources (solar, wind, hydro, etc.), whereas water is finite. What can we do to make sure we have enough for the future?

The average person in the UK uses around 150 litres of water a day. A five-minute shower uses 45 litres, a washing machine uses 50–100 litres of water and a dishwasher uses 12–20 litres of water.

And it can take more than 20,000 litres of water to produce 1kg of cotton, equivalent to a single T-shirt and a pair of jeans. For this reason, some textile manufacturers are replacing natural fabrics with material such as polyester from recycled plastic bottles.

We are consumers of both actual water and of 'virtual water'. Virtual water is the water used to make products we use or wear every day and to grow the food we eat. For example, it is estimated that 2500 litres of water are needed to produce 500g of rice, while 18,900 litres are used to produce a kilo of coffee.

Agriculture uses 70% of the world's fresh water supply for irrigation, although the percentage does vary from country to country. In some countries, industry uses far more water than agriculture.

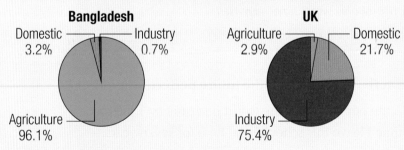

We can make a difference, provided that we act now.

2 Work in pairs. Find these words in the text and work out their meaning from the context.

1 currently
2 essential
3 finite
4 equivalent to
5 consumers

3 Use the information in the text to write questions for these answers.

1 Between 8 and 11 billion.
2 7 billion.
3 Air and water.
4 70%.
5 Around 150 litres of water a day.
6 More than 20,000 litres.
7 It's the water used to make products we use or wear every day and to grow the food we eat.

Use of English: Conjunctions

Conjunctions join phrases and clauses in a sentence.
Find these conjunctions in the text in Exercise 1:

either … or …   both … and …
whereas   although
while   provided that

4 Use conjunctions from the Use of English box to complete these sentences.

1 In the USA each person uses just under 600 litres of water per day *whereas* in Brazil the figure is just under 200 litres.

2 _____ we mend broken water pipes _____ we risk losing 40% of our fresh water.

3 In the future, it might be possible to replace fossil fuels, such as oil, coal and gas _____ we can generate enough energy from renewable sources.

4 It's important to find ways of reducing _____ domestic _____ industrial consumption of water.

5 _____ water is a global issue, individuals can make a difference.

Project: Water for the future

5 Create a poster or a webpage showing how your country gets its water.

Where does our water come from?

Dams

Reservoirs

Desalination plants

Think about the following:

- rivers and lakes
- underground water sources
- wells
- desalination plants
- reservoirs
- dams.

1 Brainstorm ideas. What do you need to find out?

2 Research the information you need.

3 Write a section for your poster on each water source.

4 Find pictures to illustrate it.

14 Cultures and customs

- **Topics** Naming customs; ceremonies and special occasions; proverbs
- **Use of English** Participle clauses; present simple passive

Boys' names

Girls' names

What's in a name?

- Which are the most popular names for people of your age? What are the most popular 'baby names' now?

Did you know?

The Japanese name *Akira* means bright and intelligent. The Arabic name *Amir* means 'prince'.

Does your name have a meaning? What is it?

Does your name exist in another language? Is it exactly the same? Does it mean the same?

Reading and speaking

1 Read about the following naming traditions. What do you think of them?

Kenya	Nigeria	Greece
The first or birth name of a child born to Swahili speakers is chosen by an elderly relative. It usually describes the baby's appearance. *Haidar*, for example, means 'strong and stout'.	Babies born in the Yoruba community are often named according to the circumstances of their birth. For example, *Bejide*, a girl's name, means 'child born in the rainy time'; *Abegunde*, for a boy, means 'born during a holiday'. When they are a little older, the children are given a name to express wishes for the future. *Titilayo*, for example, means 'eternal happiness'.	A tradition followed by many Greek families is to name the first boy in a family after his paternal grandfather and the first girl after her maternal grandmother. Consequently, a boy named *Yannis* might have several cousins also called *Yannis*. In some families, the same names have been used for hundreds of years.

Reading

2 Read the text again. Then answer the questions.

1 Find four reasons to explain why a particular name is chosen for a child.

2 Dimitrios is Greek. He has a brother, Adonis, and two sisters, Elena and Rena. Dimitrios, Adonis, Elena and Rena each have a son. All four boys are called Georgios. Can you explain why?

Speaking

3 Work in pairs. Answer these questions about names in your country.

1 When is a baby named?

2 How is the name chosen?

3 Are there fashions in names? Give examples.

4 What influences people when they choose a name for a child?

Use of English: Participle clauses

Participle clauses are like relative clauses but they have participles instead of complete verbs and no relative pronoun. They're used more often in written English than spoken English.

Babies born in the Yoruba community = Babies who are born in the Yoruba community

A tradition followed by many families = A tradition which is followed by many families

Named after its Hungarian inventor, a biro is a household object throughout the world.

4 Use the past participles of the verbs in the box to complete the sentences.

> (be) born   give   take   use   serve

1 In parts of West Africa, children are given names associated with the day on which they are born. For example, boys _____ on Monday are called Kwadwo and girls are called Adwoa.

2 Popular names _____ to children in the UK 50 years ago were Tracey for girls and Paul for boys.

3 A slice of meat between two slices of bread is a popular snack. _____ to the Earl of Sandwich in the 1760s, it became known as 'a sandwich'.

4 The description 'a Scrooge', _____ from Charles Dickens' story *A Christmas Carol*, is used of someone who doesn't like spending their money.

5 The fabric denim, _____ to make jeans, comes from the French *de Nîmes*, meaning 'from Nîmes'.

Listening (23)

5 Listen to two people talking about their names. What is the difference in their attitude towards their nicknames?

> **Language tip**
>
> A 'nickname' is an informal name that your friends or family call you. The word 'nickname' comes from Old English *an eke name*. Eke meant 'also' in Old English, so 'an eke name' was 'an extra name'.

6 Listen again and complete the chart.

First name	Name used at home	Nickname	Reason for the nickname
Thomas			
Alison			

7 There is an inconsistency in what Thomas says about what he's called and in what Alison says about what she's called. What are they? Listen again if you need to.

Speaking

8 Work in small groups. Answer these questions.

1 Do you like your name? Why? / Why not?

2 What are you called at home?

3 What do your friends call you?

4 Have you got a nickname? What's the reason for it?

Writing

9 Write a paragraph about names in your country for English students who are coming on a school exchange.

- Traditionally, how are names chosen for children?
- What are the most popular names for boys and girls and what do they mean?
- Are nicknames used in families or among friends?

Ceremonies and special occasions

- A ceremony is a formal event with special traditions, actions or words.
  Which ceremonies can you think of? What happens at these ceremonies?

Reading

1 Read the magazine article. Describe what's happening in the two pictures.

Let's celebrate!

In Japan babies between the ages of 6 months and 18 months take part in *nakizumo*, a 400-year-old tradition. The word *naki-zumo* means 'crying baby sumo'. Two babies are placed on cushions next to each other. A referee tries to make them cry. The baby who cries longest and loudest is the winner. The competition is inspired by the Japanese proverb 'crying babies grow fast'.

To mark an engagement in Pakistan, a special ceremony called a *mangni* is held. It gives the families of the future bride and groom a chance to meet. The bride's dress for the *mangni* ceremony is given by the groom's family. Traditionally, the bride is given garlands of flowers and sweet things to eat by seven married women from the groom's family. The groom is expected to propose marriage formally. Rings are exchanged and a date for the wedding is set.

In Mexico, Cuba, Puerto Rico and in Central and South America, a girl has a special party given by her parents to celebrate her 15th birthday. The girl's closest friends and family members are invited. Long dresses are worn by the girls and the boys wear formal suits. During the party, the *quinceañera* (the girl celebrating her 15th birthday) changes her flat shoes for a pair of high-heeled shoes given to her by her father. This is to mark her passage from childhood towards adulthood.

In Greece, as in many European and Latin American countries, name days are celebrated. Traditionally families held 'open house' for a family member's name day party and friends and neighbours could drop in for food and sweets. Today guests are usually invited and they bring a small gift or flowers, or they send a card.

2 Read the text messages. Each one refers to one of the ceremonies or special occasions described on page 112. Write a sentence or two about what has just happened.

1

> Thanks Mum and Dad for a lovely party. I had a wonderful time and I love the shoes.
>
> **Gabriela**

2

> Save the date! We're getting married on 22 August.
>
> **Ibrahim & Faisa**

3

> Thanks for the card. I liked the way you'd illustrated 'Katarina' on the front. I'm going to put it in a frame.
>
> **Katarina**

4

> Good news! She won! We're very proud of her.
>
> **Kurumi**

3 Work in pairs. Read the article again. Then check how much you remember.

Partner A: Choose a word or phrase from the article, for example, 'cushions'.

Partner B: Without looking at the text, explain the significance of Partner A's word or phrase in terms of the ceremonies and special occasions described in the article.

Use of English: Present simple passive

We often use the passive when describing formal occasions because it is the actions that are important, not who does them.

To mark an engagement in Pakistan, a special ceremony called a 'mangni' is held.

Rings are exchanged and a date for the wedding is set.

4 Complete the sentences with a suitable verb in the passive.

1 At a wedding ceremony, the wedding rings _____ sometimes _____ on a small cushion.

2 Promises or 'vows' _____ by a bride and groom at their wedding.

3 The traditional *qipeo* _____ often _____ in northern China as a wedding dress.

4 In Russia, flowers _____ always _____ in odd numbers.

5 To mark the occasion, a ceremony _____ every year on 11 November.

6 Today, guests _____ sometimes _____ to a name day party by a text message.

Vocabulary

5 Match the verbs and the nouns to make collocations associated with engagement and marriage. Look back to the text in Exercise 1 to help you.

  1 *to mark an engagement*

1	to mark	rings
2	to hold	an engagement
3	to propose	marriage
4	to exchange	a date
5	to set	a ceremony

6 Write a paragraph describing engagement and marriage traditions in your country. Use the phrases from Exercise 5.

Pearls of wisdom

- 'A problem shared is a problem halved' is a proverb. What is a proverb? What do you think this particular proverb means?

Proverbs and traditional sayings often contain words that rhyme or include *alliteration* (the use of words that begin with the same sound). Some are *metaphorical*: they use one idea to express another. Others are *literal*: they express an idea that is straightforward and obvious.

Here are some examples of English proverbs and sayings.

Birds of a feather flock together.

Better late than never.

An apple a day keeps the doctor away.

The early bird catches the worm.

A stitch in time saves nine.

Look before you leap.

Red sky at night, shepherd's delight.
Red sky in the morning, shepherd's warning.

Too many cooks spoil the broth.

The leopard cannot change its spots.

Once bitten, twice shy.

flock a flock is a group of birds, sheep or goats; to flock is to go somewhere in a large group

worm a long thin creature with no legs and no bones that lives in soil

leap jump high or a long distance

shepherd someone who looks after sheep

broth a thin soup, often with vegetables or rice in it

bitten the past participle of *bite*

Reading

1 Read the proverbs. Match the cartoons to three of them.

2 Answer the questions.

1 How many examples of rhyming words can you find?

2 Find examples of alliteration in the proverbs.

3 Find examples of proverbs which are both literal and metaphorical.

4 Why do you think rhyme and alliteration are a feature of many proverbs?

Speaking and writing

3 Work in pairs. Discuss what you think the proverbs above mean.

Partner A: Birds of a feather flock together. What do you think that means?

Partner B: I think it means that people who like the same things usually get on well together.

Partner A: And perhaps enjoy spending time with each other.

Partner B: Yes.

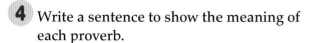

4 Write a sentence to show the meaning of each proverb.

Compare your sentences with what other students wrote. Can you improve your sentences to explain the meaning of the proverbs more clearly?

This means that people who like the same things usually get on well and enjoy spending time with each other.

5 Work in pairs. Answer the questions. Then share your ideas with the rest of the class.

1 Which of the proverbs do you think might be based on truths with a scientific basis?

2 Do you agree with these proverbs?

6 Work in pairs. Think of proverbs in your own language and answer these questions.

1 How would you translate the proverbs into English?

2 Do they have a literal or metaphorical meaning, or both?

3 Do any of them feature rhyme or alliteration?

4 Do any of them have a similar meaning to the proverbs in Exercise 1?

7 Work in pairs. Choose one of the proverbs and write a short dialogue to illustrate it but don't include the proverb. Act out your dialogue for the class. The class has to say which proverb it illustrates.

A: *There's something wrong with your computer. I think it's got a virus.*

B: *Oh, it'll be all right.*

A: *No, I think you should have it checked right now.*

B: *Don't worry. I'm sure it's fine.*

A: *If you don't get it fixed now, it will get a lot worse. It could destroy all your files!*

(A stitch in time saves nine.)

Project: Write a short story

8 Write a short story using a proverb as the title or as the final line of the story.

● Think of an idea or scenario for a story that you can match to a proverb from Exercise 1.

● You can start by setting the scene for the story: describe where it takes place and who is involved.

Too many cooks spoil the broth

It was a hot Thursday afternoon and Jessica and her friends were walking home from school.

'I want to make a special present for Alicia,' said Jessica.

'We'll help you. We can …'

…

'It's OK. I'll do it myself,' said Jessica. 'After all, too many cooks spoil the broth.'

● Or you can start with dialogue.

The football match

'The match starts in five minutes and Malik isn't here.'

'We'll just have to start without him.'

…

'Malik, where have you been? We're three nil down!'

…

'Better late than never.'

Punctuation guide for direct speech

● Use quotation marks for direct speech, that is for what people actually say:
'I'll help you,' Harry said.
You can invert the subject and verb after direct speech:
'I'll help you,' said Harry.

● For each new speaker, start a new line.
'I want to make a special present for Alicia.'
'We'll help you. We can …'

● Question marks and exclamation marks come inside the quotation marks.
'What do you want me to do?' asked Mia.

Fiction (24)

They Don't Mean It!
Lensey Namioka

1 Read the extract. It's from a short story. What is the author trying to show?

2 Read the extract again and make a list of any words you don't know.

3 Work in pairs. Compare your list with your partner's list. Have you written down the same words? Look up the meaning of any words you don't know in a dictionary.

4 Answer the questions.

1 Why does Kim gasp at what Mary's father and mother say?
2 How would you summarise the difference between Kim's attitude and Mary's attitude towards responding to compliments?
3 Had Mary and Kim noticed this difference before the party? How do you know?
4 Why is the story called 'They Don't Mean It!'?

5 Answer these questions about the style of the extract.

1 Why does the writer use three spaced asterisks (* * *) between lines 26 and 27?
2 Find four words which the writer uses instead of 'said'.
3 Why does the writer use a lot of direct speech in this extract?
4 Why does the writer put certain words in italics?
5 For which age group do you think this story is intended?

6 If you had to explain to someone visiting your country how to respond to compliments, what would you say?

They Don't Mean It!

Mary Yang and her family moved to America from China two years ago. They decide to give a party for Chinese New Year and they invite some of their friends, including the Eng family, who are also Chinese American, and Mary's American friend
5 *Kim O'Meara and her family. It's the end of the evening and the guests are thanking the Yangs for the party.*

"The fish was delicious!" Mrs Eng said to Father. "I'll have to get the recipe from your wife one of these days. She's a wonderful cook, isn't she?"

10 "Oh, no, she's not a good cook at all," said Father. "You're just being polite."

I heard a little gasp from my friend Kim. She stared wide-eyed at Father.

"What's the matter, Kim?" I asked.

15 Instead of answering, Kim turned to look at Mrs O'Meara, who was saying to my mother, "I *loved* your ten-vegetable salad. Even the kids loved it, and they don't usually eat their vegetables. You and the girls must have spent *hours* doing all that fine dicing and slicing!"

20 "The girls did the cutting, and I'm sorry they did such a terrible job," said Mother. "I'm embarrassed at how thick those pieces of celery were!"

I heard another little gasp from Kim, who was now staring at Mother. But I didn't get a chance to ask her what the
25 problem was. The O'Mearas were going out the front door, and the rest of the guests followed.

* * *

"How come your father and your mother were so nasty last night?" asked Kim when we were walking to the school bus stop the next morning.

30 "What do you mean?" I asked. I didn't remember Father or Mother acting nasty.

"It was when Mrs Eng was telling your dad what a good cook your mom is," replied Kim.

That's right. Mrs Eng did say something about Mother being a good cook. "So what's bothering you?" I asked. 35

Kim stopped dead. "Didn't you hear your dad?" she demanded. "He said that your mom wasn't a good cook at all, and that Mrs Eng was just being polite!"

I still didn't understand why Kim was bothered. "So what? People are always saying things like that." 40

But Kim wasn't finished. "And then when my mom said how hard you worked to cut up the vegetables, your mom said she was embarrassed by what a terrible job you did in slicing!"

I had to laugh. "She doesn't mean it! It's just the way she 45 talks."

When the school bus arrived and we got on, Kim began again. "Then why do your parents keep saying these bad things if they don't mean it? I'd be really hurt if my mom said I did a terrible job – after I worked so hard, too." 50

What Kim said made me thoughtful. I suddenly realised that whenever people said good things about us, my parents always contradicted them and said how bad we really were. We kids knew perfectly well that our parents didn't mean it, so our feelings weren't hurt in the least. It was just the way 55 Chinese parents were supposed to talk.

Finally I said to Kim, "I think that if my parents agreed with the compliments, then that would be the same as bragging. It's good manners to contradict people when they compliment your children." 60

"It's bragging only if you say good things about *yourself*," protested Kim. "It's different when your parents are talking about *you*."

I shook my head. "We Chinese feel it's the same thing. Boasting about our children, or husband, or wife, is the same 65 as boasting about ourselves. People even think it's bad luck."

by Lensey Namioka

Review of Units 13–14

Vocabulary

People and places

1 Label the regions of this country using the following terms:

densely populated

moderately populated

sparsely populated

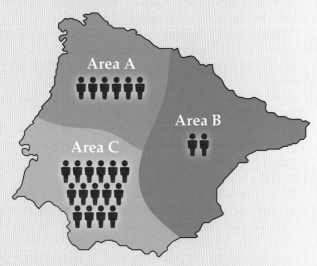

2 Put the words in the box in the following categories.

relief	climate	vegetation	resources

coal	rainforest
grassland	temperate
hill	trees
hot	tropical
minerals	valley
mountain	water
oil	wet
plants	wood

3 Complete the text with the words from the list.

birth rate   life expectancy   sector
immigration   population

Italy has a _____¹ of 61 million. It has the highest _____² in the European Union, 80 years for men and 85 for women. Until the 1980s, Italy was a homogeneous society in terms of culture and language. Since then _____³ has increased. Today, immigrants make up almost 10% of the population. There is serious concern about the dramatically declining _____⁴: fewer babies were born in Italy in 2014 than in any other year since Italy became a unified state in 1861. This has serious implications for every _____⁵ but especially for the economy and for health.

Ceremonies and special occasions

4 Choose the correct option.

1 They *made / did / held* a ceremony to which family and close friends were invited.

2 They *marked / showed / presented* their engagement with a special celebration.

3 The bride and groom *transferred / exchanged / changed* rings.

4 The groom formally *proposed / advised / suggested* marriage.

5 They *marked / set / put* a date for the wedding.

Proverbs

5 Match the two halves of the proverbs.

1	An apple a day	a	catches the worm.
2	The early bird	b	change its spots.
3	A stitch in time	c	keeps the doctor away.
4	Look before you	d	leap.
5	Too many cooks	e	saves nine.
6	The leopard cannot	f	spoil the broth.

Which proverb means 'If a lot of people try to help to do a job, it can cause problems'?

Use of English

6 Complete the sentences using the verbs in brackets in the future perfect.

1 By 2050, the number of people over the age of 65 (*increase*) will have increased to 15.9% of the total world population.

2 The percentage of people between the ages of 15 and 64 (*rise*) to 64%.

3 By contrast, the percentage of people under the age of 14 (*fall*) to 2.1%.

4 The European Union's population (*grow*) to more than 520 million by 2035; however, by 2060 it (*decline*) to 505 million.

7 Complete each sentence with the correct conjunction.

although	whereas	provided that
either ... or	both ... and	

1 _____ you can send a card for a friend's name day, it is more common today to send a text.

2 You can _____ take flowers _____ take a present, such as a box of chocolates.

3 In some countries, such as Russia, you can give flowers _____ you give an odd number of flowers, not an even number.

4 In Spain and Latin America, everyone has two surnames, for example *García Márquez* and *Vargas Llosa*. This is because people use _____ their mother's _____ their father's surnames.

5 In Kenya, the first name of a child born to Swahili speakers describes its appearance, _____ in Nigeria, babies are named according to the circumstances of their birth.

General knowledge quiz

8 Work in pairs. Ask and answer the questions.

1 In which country are the cities Manaus, Recife and São Paulo?

2 For which material did Manaus become famous in the 19th century?

3 Which part of Brazil is the most densely populated: the south-east, the central area or the north-west?

4 What is the population of the world: 5 billion, 7 billion or 11 billion?

5 What is Swahili?

6 Where are the Yoruba people from?

7 In which country is there a 400-year-old tradition called *nakizumo* and what is it?

8 Name one country or area where a girl has a special party to celebrate her 15th birthday?

9 Complete this proverb: 'Red sky at night. ...'. What does it mean?

10 Which proverb does this photo illustrate?

15 The digital age

- **Topics** Using print and digital resources; developments in technology; the advantages and disadvantages of digital technology
- **Use of English** Prepositional and phrasal verbs to do with using technology, *log in*, *click on*, etc.; focusing adverbs, *only*, *just*, *simply*, etc.; adverbs of degree, *extremely*, *quite*, etc.

Zoom in!

- What do you write by hand? In the future, do you think children will need to learn to handwrite?

Speaking

1 Work in pairs. Discuss the advantages and disadvantages of using each of the following:

The main advantage of using a pencil is that ...
One of the disadvantages is that ...

a pencil

a fountain pen

a biro

a smartphone

2 Copy and complete the chart. Add ticks to the columns to show how much you use paper and how much you use digital resources.

	Paper	Digital
diary		
calendar		
photos		
messages to friends, notes, cards, etc.		
school textbooks		
homework		
reference books, e.g. dictionaries		
reading for pleasure:		
books		
magazines		

3 Work in pairs. Use your chart to ask each other questions. What are the similarities and differences between you?

> Do you use a diary? What sort of diary do you use?

> When you read for pleasure, do you use an e-reader or do you prefer printed books?

> Do you use an online dictionary?

Listening (25)

4 Listen to two phone conversations. What is the reason for each call?

5 Listen again. Complete the phrases and sentences with the correct words.

1 Every time I try to attach a _____ to an email ...
2 ... the _____ freezes.
3 Have you backed up your hard _____ recently?
4 Hold down the on / off _____ for five seconds.
5 I want to download the application _____.
6 And have you logged in to the sports centre _____?
7 I've typed in my _____.
8 You need to scroll down, right to the bottom of the _____.
9 Click on the _____.
10 You can zoom in on the _____.
11 You can fill in the form _____.
12 You can print it out and keep a _____.

Use of English: Prepositional and phrasal verbs to do with using technology

When you talk about using a computer, you often use a verb followed by a preposition / adverbial particle. For example, we attach a document to an email and we back up our hard disk.

Find eight more verbs followed by prepositions / adverbial particles in the phrases and sentences in Exercise 5.

6 Complete each sentence with an appropriate verb followed by a preposition / adverbial particle.

1 Be careful, this computer often crashes so remember to _____ _____ your work.
2 I don't _____ _____ many documents because it's a waste of paper.
3 This is the airline's website address. You'll need to _____ _____ to the website and _____ _____ your password before you can confirm your flight.
4 It's hard to find the contact telephone number on this webpage but if you _____ _____ you'll find it at the bottom.
5 I think it's you in the background of the photo. _____ _____ on that top corner and we'll be able to see.
6 Which symbol do I _____ _____ to reply to an email?
7 To get an accent over the e of *café*, _____ _____ the alt key and press e. Then press e again.

7 Write a note to explain to someone who hasn't used your computer before how to switch it on and open a document. What should they do if the screen freezes?

That's a good idea!

- What are the most exciting recent developments in technology?

Reading

1 Read the magazine article. Which of the following would you choose as the title?

Robots are taking over the world   Technology for the environment   Making good use of technology

Robots deliver dishes to customers at a Robot Restaurant in Harbin, Heilongjiang province in China. Opened in June 2012, the restaurant has become famous for its 20 robots. The robots are between 1.3 and 1.6 metres tall. They don't only deliver dishes to the table, they also cook meals. They are able to display over ten expressions on their faces and say basic welcoming sentences to customers. They can work continuously for five hours after a two-hour charge. They are very popular, particularly with children.

What is 'wearable technology'? Is it just gadgets like smartwatches and fitness monitors? Designer Lauren Bowker has other ideas. She has developed a range of clothing that reacts to biological and chemical stimulus.

Her clothes include pieces that change colour depending on changes in the environment or stimulation from the brain.

One of her pieces is made of leather and changes colour in reaction to wind and air. Originally Lauren thought this type of technology could be used for Formula 1 racing in order to assess the aerodynamics of vehicles, but then she began developing clothes designed to reflect the way wind and air pass over the human body.

Another of her pieces reacts to heat in the brain and therefore changes colour depending on your thoughts. Lauren says that in the future, she hopes there will be no need for disposable fashion, as one garment will simply adapt to be suitable for all situations, moods and weather.

2 Work in pairs. Find the following words in the text and work out their meaning from the context.

1 display
2 basic
3 continuously
4 aerodynamics
5 disposable
6 garment
7 adapt

3 Read the text again and complete each of the following sentences with an appropriate word.

1 The robots range in _____ from 1.3 to 1.6 metres.

2 The robots are both cooks _____ waiters.

3 _____ the robots can speak to the customers, they can only say a few simple things.

4 The robots can work for five hours _____ needing to be recharged.

5 Lauren Bowker is _____ in designing clothes not gadgets.

6 Lauren applied this type of technology to fashion _____ trying to apply it to racing cars.

7 Lauren looks forward to the time when people will not throw away their clothes _____ they will only need one garment.

Use of English: Focusing adverbs

Focusing adverbs focus your attention on a thing or an action. They include:

especially   generally   mainly   even   only   just   particularly   simply

They don't only deliver dishes to the table, they also cook meals.

The robots are very popular, particularly with children.

Is it just gadgets like smartwatches and fitness monitors?

One garment will simply adapt to be suitable for all situations, moods and weather.

4 Rewrite the sentences using the words in brackets.

1 We all love gadgets, but my brother loves them more than the rest of us.
(*especially*) We all love gadgets, especially my brother.

2 It's usually true that children are better than their parents with new technology.
(*generally*) Children _____.

3 The special vests that footballers wear to track their movements are useful for assessing fitness and agility more than for anything else.
(*particularly*) The special vests _____.

4 Amazingly, this new robot can read!
(*even*) This new robot _____.

5 Almost all of Lauren Bowker's fans are under 30.
(*mainly*) Lauren Bowker's fans _____.

Speaking

5 Work in small groups. Discuss the following.

1 What are the advantages and disadvantages of robots working as waiters?

2 What are the advantages and disadvantages of robots working as cooks?

3 Apart from restaurants, in which other places could robots work? (Discuss the advantages and disadvantages.)

4 What kind of work could a robot do around the house?

5 Would you like to wear the clothes that Lauren Bowker designs? Why? Why not?

6 If you could commission a design from Lauren, what would it be?

The future is digital

● How do you differ from your parents in your attitude to digital devices?

Listening 26

1 You will hear an interview with Richard Evans, an educational psychologist, about how children and teenagers use digital devices. How would you describe Richard's attitude? How would you describe the interviewer's attitude?

2 Listen again. For each question choose A, B or C.

1 Richard thinks children and teenagers today:
   A spend too much time with digital devices
   B are not as fortunate as children in his generation
   C are used to using several digital devices at the same time.

2 According to the research Richard has done:
   A young people find it difficult to concentrate on their homework
   B computers and other devices can help young people with their studies
   C young people depend on the Internet to do their homework.

3 Richard thinks that:
   A books are a better source of information than the Internet because it's more difficult to copy from them
   B students should check the information they take from websites and make sure they understand it
   C people in his generation learned more effectively than students today.

4 On the topic of technology and very young children, Richard:
   A thinks that technology can have a bad effect on very young children
   B thinks that very young children should not be allowed to use a tablet or similar device
   C thinks it's a good thing that children get to grips with technology at an early age.

5 Richard thinks that:
   A it's right that people should be worried about Internet addiction
   B young people spend too much time on social media when they should be spending time with friends
   C young people are more fortunate now than when he was young.

Use of English: Adverbs of degree

Adverbs of degree modify adjectives or other adverbs.

Parents are extremely concerned about the amount of time their teenage children are spending on digital devices.

They find it quite hard to concentrate.

It's a bit sad!

I think these fears have been rather exaggerated.

I can remember being totally bored for a lot of my teenage years!

Extremely and *totally* are like *very* but they're stronger.

Quite can mean 'a bit' or it can mean 'very', depending on how you say it and how you say the word that follows it.

Rather is stronger than *quite*.

3 Complete these sentences to make them true for you and to give your views. Then compare them with what other members of the class have written.

1 I find it quite hard to …
2 I think it's a bit sad when …
3 Some people are extremely concerned about …
4 Fears about … are rather exaggerated.
5 I was totally bored when …

Speaking

4 Work in small groups. Read these statements. Give your own opinion, supported with examples. Say whether you agree or disagree with what others say.

1 Teenagers spend too much time using digital devices.
2 You shouldn't try to listen to music, check messages and play video games when you're doing your homework.
3 We shouldn't take information directly from the Internet for our school work.
4 Children under 5 should not be given digital devices.
5 Internet addiction is a real problem for people of all ages.

Project: Write a report for a technology magazine

5 Write a report of a development in technology that interests you.

1 Share your idea with others.

- What is it?
- How does it work?
- Who might use it?
- Why do you think it's a good idea?

a kit to build your own robot

an app for keeping and organising notes and information for school work

a digital sketchbook

software for making and editing videos

software for composing and recording music

2 Write your report. Ask others to comment on it and check it.

- **Topics** Optical illusions; the perception of colour; sounds in language
- **Use of English** Prepositional phrases; conjunctions followed by *-ing* forms

A trick of the light

- An illusion is something that is not really what it seems to be. Why is illusion important in plays and films?

Reading

1 Read the article. Why is 'Pepper's ghost' a trick of the light?

Did you know?

In 350 BCE, the philosopher Aristotle wrote that 'our senses can be trusted but they can easily be fooled'.

He gave the example of watching a waterfall. If, after a time, you look at the rocks beside the water, they appear to move in the opposite direction to the water.

This is called 'the waterfall illusion' or 'motion after-effect'.

Can you think of a situation in which you have noticed a similar effect?

Pepper's GHOST, *then* and *now*

Pepper's ghost is the name of an optical illusion which was popular in the theatre in the mid-nineteenth century. Named after John Henry Pepper, it was a way of making an unreal figure or 'ghost' appear on the stage. This is how it works.

If you've ever looked at your reflection in a shop window on a dark night, you will have seen a version of Pepper's ghost. And you may have seen it at the theatre. The trick is to place a large sheet of glass at an angle between the actors and the audience. By using the stage lights in just the right way, the glass becomes

Speaking

2 Work in pairs. Look at the picture of Pepper's ghost. Describe what it is and how it works without looking at the text.

Language tip

Notice that after *not only*, the verb comes before the subject:

Not only can the stage be seen through the glass, but so can anything placed in the right position where the glass is pointing.

NOT

Not only ~~the stage can~~ …

a half mirror. Not only can the stage be seen through the glass, but so can anything placed in the right position where the glass is facing. Because of the way light is reflected, the reflected image – the 'ghost' – doesn't seem to be on the surface of the glass; it seems to be on the stage. The actor playing the ghost performs in an area at the side of the stage or below it, hidden from the audience. When it is time for the ghost to appear, a very strong light is shone on the actor. Suddenly, his or her reflection appears on the stage. To make the ghost disappear, the light is simply switched off. The illusion was premiered in a production of Charles Dickens' *The Haunted Man* in 1862.

Since then, Pepper's idea of projecting images has been widely used in theme parks, films and concerts. In South Korea today, concerts in which holograms of singers and dancers are projected onto a large stage are a top attraction in Seoul. Technology has brought Pepper's ghost into the twenty-first century.

The Japanese pianist Yoshiki plays with a hologram version of himself. The audience was amazed when the hologram appeared first, and then introduced the real performer!

Use of English: Prepositional phrases

Certain prepositions are commonly combined with certain nouns:

What's on at the theatre?

NOT

~~in the theatre?~~

3 Complete the sentences with the correct prepositions.

1 He got a shock when he saw his reflection _____ the shop window.

2 The first scene of the play opens _____ a dark night in Verona.

3 It's great to see films with lots of special effects _____ the cinema.

4 Do you think the sheet of glass is meant to be _____ an angle or should it be straight?

5 Singers and actors have to learn how to use their voices _____ just the right way so that they don't damage them.

6 Before the curtain goes up, everything has to be _____ the right position on the stage.

Writing

4 You were at the theatre and saw the play shown in the picture in Exercise 1. You were amazed. Write a description for your diary of what you saw. Describe what was happening on the stage …

… before the illusion appeared

… when the illusion appeared

… after the illusion disappeared

This evening I saw an amazing play at the theatre. In one of the scenes, …

How we see the world

● How many colours can you see in your classroom? Do you all agree on the colours of the objects around you?

Listening

1 Look at this dress. What colour is it? Listen to the radio news. Why is the dress the subject of a news item?

2 Listen again and answer the questions.

1 Why did Cecilia Bleasdale buy the dress?

2 When she sent a photo of the dress to her daughter Grace, what was her reaction? What did Keir think?

3 What did Grace's friend Caitlin do and what was the result?

4 What did most people think the colour of the dress was?

5 Why do some people see the dress as white and gold?

6 Why do other people see the dress as blue and black?

Reading

3 Work in pairs. Read the following text. Which of the pieces of information did you already know?

The science of colour

Research shows that colour really does affect our minds and bodies. The colour blue helps us to feel calm. Red, on the other hand, can make us feel angry. Football teams seem to play better when wearing red. They are more likely to win matches than those wearing other colours.

After analysing recent sales of works of art, a leading expert concluded that pictures with red in them fetch higher prices than those without.

Colour is how our eyes interpret light. It is the way our brain perceives mixtures of different light wavelengths falling on the retina of the eyes. Human vision is trichromatic. We have three different colour receptors (cones) in our eyes, each designed to pick up different wavelengths of light. These are red, green and blue. People who are colour-blind only have two kinds of receptors, meaning they can only detect green and blue wavelengths.

There are people who are 'tetrachromatic', which means they have an extra cone type in their eyes. The average person can see approximately 1 million colours, whereas people who have tetrachromatic vision can see 99 million.

Birds are also tetrachromatic – they have four colour receptors and see things that we see as red as many different shades of colour. This is very useful for them while searching for food.

4 Read the text again. Match each of the following headings to a paragraph.

a By using certain colours, painters can sell their work for more money.

b Colour does not exist in the external world.

c It is thought that emotions are stimulated by certain colours.

d Some animals are better than humans at seeing colours.

e Some people can see more colours than others.

5 Work in pairs. Read the text once more. Then close your book. Which of the facts can you remember? Tell your partner.

6 Complete these sentences using one of the following conjunctions followed by the verb in brackets in the -*ing* form.

| after | before | when | while | since |

1 I always read for half an hour _____ (*go*) to sleep.

2 I'm not surprised you feel sick _____ (*eat*) all that ice cream.

3 She's become much more confident _____ (*start*) at a new school.

4 Please remember to take all your things with you _____ (*leave*) the exam room.

5 Can you concentrate on your homework _____ (*listen*) to music?

Speaking

7 Work in small groups.

1 Look at picture 1. What can you say about the colour of the squares marked A and B? (Remember that our perception of colour is affected by context.) Cover the areas to the right and left of squares A and B to find the answer.

2 Look at picture 2. What colour are the two squares? Now cover the background colours and put your finger across the middle to cover the dividing line between the two squares. What do you notice?

> ### Use of English: Conjunctions followed by -*ing* forms
>
> Conjunctions are words that join clauses together in a sentence.
>
> Some conjunctions are followed by –*ing* forms.
>
> *Football teams seem to play better when wearing red.*
>
> *After analysing recent sales of works of art, a leading expert concluded that pictures with red in them fetch higher prices than those without.*
>
> *This is very useful for them while searching for food.*

1

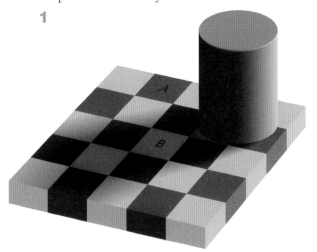

2

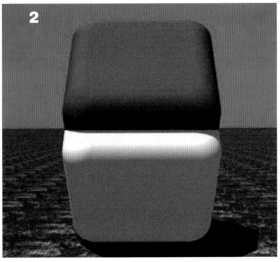

Sounds good to me!

- What kind of sounds put your teeth on edge (make you feel really uncomfortable)? What are your favourite sounds?

Reading

Onomatopoeic words are words which sound like the sound they describe.

For example, a cat *miaows*, a snake *hisses*, a big bell *clangs* and a small bell *tinkles*.

1 The words in red are all onomatopoeic. Match the words in the two columns.

I can hear …

the roar	an apple
tyres	banging
a door	buzzing in the flowerbeds
rain	of the traffic
the distant rumble	of thunder
leaves	pattering on the roof
children shrieking	screeching
bees	with laughter
someone crunching	rustling in the wind

Listening 28

2 Listen and check your answers to Exercise 1.

Speaking

3 Work in pairs. Which of the sounds in Exercise 1 have you heard today? Tell your partner.

Reading

4 Read this extract from a book on English vocabulary.

Particular combinations of letters have particular sound associations in English.

gr- at the beginning of a word can suggest something unpleasant or miserable, e.g. **groan** [make a deep sound forced out by pain or despair], **grumble** [complain in a bad-tempered way], **grumpy** [bad-tempered], **growl** [make a low, threatening sound].

cl- at the beginning of a word can suggest something sharp and / or metallic, e.g. **click** [make a short sharp sound], **clang** [make a loud ringing noise], **clank** [make a dull metallic noise, not as loud as a clang], **clash** [make a loud, broken, confused noise as when metal objects strike together]. Horses go **clip-clop** on the road.

sp- at the beginning of a word can have an association with water or other liquids or powders, e.g. **splash** [cause a liquid to fly about in drops], **spit** [send liquid out from the mouth], **splutter** [make a series of spitting sounds], **spray** [liquid sent through the air in tiny drops either by the wind or some instrument], **sprinkle** [throw a shower of something onto a surface].

-ash at the end of a word can suggest something fast and violent, e.g. **smash** [break violently into small pieces], **dash** [move or be moved violently], **crash** [strike suddenly violently and noisily], **bash** [strike heavily so as to break or injure].

wh- at the beginning of a word often suggests the movement of air, e.g. **whistle** [a high-pitched noise made by forcing air or steam through a small opening], **whirr** [sound like a bird's wings moving rapidly], **whizz** [make the sound of something rushing through the air].

-ckle, **-ggle**, or **-zzle** at the end of a word can suggest something light and repeated, e.g. **trickle** [to flow in a thin stream], **crackle** [make a series of short cracking sounds], **tinkle** [make a succession of light ringing sounds], **giggle** [laugh lightly in a nervous or silly way], **wriggle** [move with quick short twistings], **sizzle** [make a hissing sound like something cooking in fat], **drizzle** [small, fine rain].

5 Complete these sentences with a suitable onomatopoeic word from the text in Exercise 4. Remember to put it in the correct form.

1 You're always complaining about how much you've got to do. Stop _____ and just get on with it!

2 Cheer up and stop being so _____!

3 Double-_____ on the mouse to open the attachment.

4 When the cymbals _____ at the end of the symphony, I almost jumped out of my seat.

5 When we go to the seaside, we love to run into the sea and _____ water all over each other.

6 Before eating a pancake, it's nice to _____ sugar and a few drops of lemon juice over it.

7 I came downstairs too quickly, tripped, knocked my aunt's Ming vase off the shelf and _____ it to pieces.

8 The bamboo stick _____ through the air like an arrow.

9 The wood for the campfire was so dry that it _____ into life as soon as we put a match to it.

10 You could hear the meat _____ on the barbecue.

Speaking

6 Work in small groups. Invent a story. One person in the group starts by making up a sentence including one of the onomatopoeic words on these pages. Each person in the group takes it in turn to add a sentence to the story, using an onomatopoeic word.

Project

7 Write the story your group made up in Exercise 6. You can change the details if you like but make sure it includes a lot of the onomatopoeic words.

● Write a draft of your story.

● Give your story to another member of your group to comment on and check.

● Write the final version of your story.

> **Did you know?**
>
> Cats have much better hearing than humans. They can hear ultrasonic frequencies that are beyond the upper limit of the human hearing range. What's more, a cat can turn its ears in the direction of a sound, which helps when hunting prey.

Poetry

The Sound Collector
SSHH!

1 (29) Listen and read. Which of the two poems has a more regular rhythm?

2 Read the poems again and answer these questions.

1 What does the poet want us to focus on in *The Sound Collector*?

2 What does the poet want us to focus on in *SSHH!*?

3 Does *The Sound Collector* rely more on the sound of words than on the images they create? Is the same true of *SSHH!*?

4 What can you say about the rhyme scheme of each poem? Look at the words at the end of each line.

5 What do you think the message of each poem is?

3 Answer these questions about the style of the two poems.

The Sound Collector

1 Find examples of onomatopoeic words in *The Sound Collector*.

2 Why does the poet use so many onomatopoeic words in this poem?

3 Apart from the final full stop, there is no punctuation in the poem. Why?

SSHH!

4 Which of the similes in the poem *SSHH!* do you think best conveys the idea of quietness?

5 Why do you think the poet has chosen to write the poem in verses of two lines rather than as one long verse?

6 Why is SHOUT in capital letters in the last line?

4 Discuss this question: Which of the two poems do you find more memorable and why?

5 Write another two-line verse starting with '*Quiet as …*' to add to *SSHH!*

> Remember that *onomatopoeic* words are words which sound like the sound they describe.
>
> For example, in *The Sound Collector*, the kitten (a young cat) is *purring*. A cat makes a noise that sounds like *purr* when it is contented, so *purr* is an onomatopoeic word.
>
> A *simile* describes something by comparing it to something else, using *like* or *as*. For example, (*As*) *quiet as the daytime creeping in* in line 1 of *SSHH!* is a simile.

The Sound Collector

Roger McGough

A stranger called this morning
Dressed all in black and grey
Put every sound into a bag
And carried them away

5 The whistling of the kettle
The turning of the lock
The purring of the kitten
The ticking of the clock

The popping of the toaster
10 The crunching of the flakes
When you spread the marmalade
The scraping noise it makes

The hissing of the frying-pan
The ticking of the grill
15 The bubbling of the bathtub
As it starts to fill

The drumming of the raindrops
On the window-pane
When you do the washing-up
20 The gurgle of the drain

The crying of the baby
The squeaking of the chair
The swishing of the curtain
The creaking of the stair

25 A stranger called this morning
He didn't leave his name
Left us only silence
Life will never be the same.

SSHH!

Les Baynton

Quiet as the daytime creeping in,
Or someone dropping a tiny pin

Quiet as a painting starting to dry,
Or the footsteps of a walking fly

5 Quiet as a glider soaring in the sky,
Or the lashes fluttering across your eye

Quiet as an owl swooping in the night,
Or a beautiful butterfly's very first flight

Quiet as a memory, a sorrow, a fear,
10 Or a wonderful dream, right inside here

Quietness is precious, so seek it out,
But when you find it...please don't SHOUT!

pin

glider a light plane without an engine
soaring moving quickly and smoothly in the sky

lashes

fluttering moving quickly and gently in the air
sorrow a feeling of great sadness

Review of Units 15–16

Vocabulary

Digital devices

1 **Complete the words.**

1 When your screen does this, nothing moves and you can't change anything. It fr_____.

2 When your computer does this, the screen goes black and you might have lost some work. It cr_____.

3 You press this to switch the computer on or off. The on / off b_____.

4 It contains all your computer programs and documents. The h_____ d_____.

5 When you want to save a document or file into the computer's memory, from the Internet for example, you do this. You d_____ it.

2 **Choose the correct option.**

1 Oh no! My computer's crashed and I hadn't backed *in / up* my work.

2 When you're travelling you don't have to print *out / down* your boarding pass. You can just show it on your smartphone.

3 Type *in / off* your password, but don't let anyone see it.

4 You'll find the details you need if you scroll *in / down* to the bottom of the webpage.

5 The type is very small but if you zoom *in / on* you'll be able to read it easily.

6 To get more information, click *to / on* the link at the top of the page.

7 To get the euro symbol, hold *down / on* the 'alt' key and press '2'.

8 Remember to switch *off / out* your computer at the end of the day.

Onomatopoeic words

3 **Use the letters in the circles to write the missing words.**

1 I heard the distant (l u m b e r) of thunder.

2 The gate was (g a n b i n g) in the wind.

3 Insects were (g u z b i n z) around my head.

4 The leaves were (s l u r t i n g) in the trees.

5 I suddenly heard the (a r o r) of a lion.

Use of English

4 **Put the words in brackets in the correct place in the sentences.**

1 E-readers can be very practical, when you're going on holiday. (*especially*)

2 I buy CDs from time to time but I download music. (*generally*)

3 I've got a desktop computer but I use my laptop. (*mainly*)

4 This new fitness monitor is great. It talks to you! (*even*)

5 These robots cook food, they serve it as well. (*not only*)

6 You type in your destination to find the best route. (*just*)

7 When you're travelling, online dictionaries are useful. (*particularly*)

8 Anybody can use this camera. You switch it on and start taking photos. (*simply*)

5 One word or phrase in each sentence is in the wrong place. Rewrite the sentences putting them in the correct places.

1 She worked hard extremely so she deserved to do well.

2 I like painting quite but I prefer photography.

3 I found English pronunciation a difficult at first bit.

4 I enjoyed rather taking photos with Mum's old camera.

5 The audience totally was amazed by the optical illusion.

6 Complete the text with the correct prepositions.

I was on my way to see a play _____¹ the theatre when I noticed an interesting display _____² a shop window. There was a mirror and a painting positioned _____³ an angle so that you could see its reflection _____⁴ the mirror. If you stood _____⁵ just the right place, you could also see yourself reflected, as if you were part of the painting. It was very strange!

7 Join these sentences using the conjunctions in brackets followed by the *-ing* form of the verb.

1 Remember to save your work. Then switch off your computer. (before)

2 You can charge your phone. You can do your homework at the same time. (while)

3 I appeared in the school play. I feel more confident. (since)

4 I read the article about colours. I looked at colours in a different way. (after)

5 Fill in this application form. Please write in capital letters. (when)

General knowledge quiz

8 Work in pairs. Ask and answer the questions.

1 What do you call a machine that can move and do some of the work of a person, and is usually controlled by a computer?

2 What do you call the scientific study of how objects such as aeroplanes move through the air?

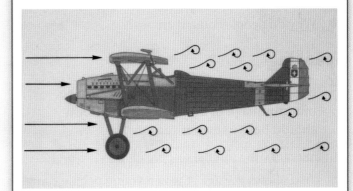

3 Where might you see Pepper's ghost?

4 What is the connection between Pepper's ghost and Charles Dickens' play *The Haunted Man*?

5 Football teams seem to play better when wearing blue. True or false?

6 Paintings which contain a certain colour tend to sell for more money than paintings without that colour. What is the colour?

7 Where is your retina?

8 How many different colour receptors do you have in your eyes?

9 Approximately how many colours can the average person see?

10 Birds are tetrachromatic. What does this mean?

Right and wrong

- **Topics** Crime; moral responsibility and citizenship
- **Use of English** Prepositional verbs to do with crime; the third conditional

Crime and punishment

- Why do people commit crimes?

Speaking

1 Look at the chart. What do you think the minimum age of criminal responsibility should be? Give your reasons.

> I think it should be ... because at that age you know the difference between right and wrong.

> I don't agree. I think that's too young. Imagine, for example, a situation in which a child's older brother asks them to ...

Minimum age of criminal responsibility

The chart shows the age at which young people can be convicted of criminal offences in certain countries.

15	15	15	14	14	12	10	10	8
the Philippines	Finland	Sweden	Japan	Vietnam	the Netherlands	Switzerland	England, Wales, Northern Ireland	Scotland

United Kingdom

2 Read the vocabulary box and complete it using these words and phrases.

> thief   attacker   car   assaulting   robbery   shop   steal   arsonist

The vocabulary of crime

Crime	Meaning	Criminal	Verb
arson	setting fire to something, especially a building, in order to damage or destroy it	*arsonist* ¹	to set fire to
assault	attacking someone physically	_____ ²	to assault / attack
theft	taking something that belongs to someone else and keeping it	_____ ³	to steal
shoplifting	taking something from a _____ ⁴ without paying for it	shoplifter	to shoplift
burglary	going into a building to _____ ⁵ things	burglar	to burgle
_____ ⁶	stealing from someone or from a place (armed robbery = using guns, knives, etc)	(armed) robber	to rob
joyriding	stealing a _____ ⁷ or other vehicle and driving it fast and dangerously for fun	joyrider	to joyride
mugging	_____ ⁸ someone in a public place in order to steal from them	mugger	to mug

Listening 🔘30

3 Listen. What has happened? Choose one of the following sentences for each person. Two of the sentences are not needed.

a He / She has been burgled.

b His / her wallet has been stolen.

c A phone has been stolen from a shop.

d He / She has been mugged.

e His / Her car has been stolen by a joyrider.

f A building has been set on fire.

4 Listen again. These pictures show what happened in three of the situations in Exercise 3. However, one detail in each picture is incorrect. What is wrong in each picture?

Reading

5 Read the newspaper extracts. Two of the crimes were featured in the reports you heard in Exercise 3. Which are they?

1

> A 24-year-old man appeared in court yesterday charged with assaulting a teenager and stealing a mobile phone in the Westway Shopping Centre on 24 June. He pleaded guilty to six similar charges of obtaining money and other valuables from members of the public. He was convicted of seven counts of theft and sentenced to six months in prison.

2

> A 21-year-old man appeared at Norwood Magistrates Court accused of breaking into a car in Norwood and driving it at high speed around the inner-city ring road. He was fined £200 for joyriding and given ten weeks' community service.

3

> Yesterday, at Nottingham Crown Court, a 21-year-old man was tried for arson. He had pleaded innocent but was found guilty. He was sent to prison for two years.

Use of English: Prepositional verbs to do with crime

When you talk about crime, you often use a verb followed by a preposition. For example, we accuse someone of a crime and we sentence someone to a period of time in prison. Here are some examples:

to charge (someone) with (a crime)

to plead guilty to (a crime)

to convict someone of (a crime)

to send someone to prison

to be tried for (a crime)

to fine someone for (doing something wrong)

Speaking

6 Work in small groups. Read the newspaper reports in Exercise 5 again. In each case, did the punishment fit the crime? Discuss.

Try to include the verbs in the Use of English box.

He had mugged seven people, he was convicted of theft and he was only sentenced to six months in prison. I don't think that's enough.

Doing the right thing

- Is it always easy to do the right thing?

Reading

1 Read these posts. What do they have in common?

What would you have done?

I was in the supermarket when I saw an old lady. She looked very poor and I saw her put a loaf of bread under her coat and leave the shop without paying. I didn't know what to do. If I'd told the store manager, he would have called the police. What would you have done?

Rona

❝*I would have paid for the loaf of bread. We should always help people less fortunate than ourselves.***❞**

One day after lessons, I was walking across the school football field on my way home when I saw some money on the ground. It was quite a lot. I picked it up but then I didn't know what to do with it. The school was closed so I couldn't go back there. In the end, I just left it where I'd found it. What would you have done if you'd been in my position?

Brandon

I had a drink and a sandwich at a café in town. When I had finished, I paid the bill and left the café. I was waiting at the bus stop when I realised I had only been charged for one item, not two. I remembered that the waitress who had served me was quite young and clearly new to the job. I could have gone back to the café but I could see my bus coming and I didn't want to miss it because there wasn't another bus for three hours. So I got on the bus and went home thinking I'd go back to the café when I was next in town. But I did worry that the girl in the café might have got into trouble. What would you have done?

Bella

We had an end-of-year Maths test two weeks ago. We knew it was going to be really hard. My best friend had been in the Maths room one lunch time and had seen the test on the teacher's laptop. He's got a photographic memory so he could remember nearly everything he had seen. He told me but nobody else. He did really well in the test, much better than the rest of us. He really needed a good mark otherwise the school would have made him repeat the year. Should I have told him to go to the Maths teacher and say that he'd seen the test? What would you have done?

Ismael

2 How would you describe the attitude of the people who have written the posts?

3 Match the sentence halves and write the complete sentences using the third conditional. Use *would have*, *could have* and *might have* as appropriate.

1 If I (buy) a ticket for my journey,
2 If he (plead) guilty,
3 If the police (not stop) them,
4 If you (not leave) your bag on the seat,
5 If we (not leave) the window open,
6 (he / pass) the exam

  a he (get) a lighter sentence.
  b I (not get) a fine.
  c if he (not see) the questions on the teacher's laptop?
  d the burglar (not get in) to the house.
  e the thief (not steal) it.
  f they (steal) the car.

Use of English: The third conditional

We use the third conditional to talk about imagined situations in the past – things that did not happen.

Clause 1	Clause 2
If + past perfect	*would have* *could have* + past participle *might have*

If I'd told the store manager, he would have called the police.
(But I didn't tell the store manager ... the situation is imaginary.)

You can reverse the order of the clauses:

If you had been in my position, what would you have done?

What would you have done if you'd been in my position?

Speaking

4 Work in pairs. Discuss what you would have done in the situations described in Exercise 1. Use *I would have ... / I wouldn't have ... / I might have ...*

A: *If I'd been in Rona's situation, I would have followed the old lady and given her some money.*

B: *But if you'd done that, she might have been very embarrassed.*

Writing

5 Look at the cartoon and continue the story.

get up earlier ➔ not miss the school bus	not have mobile phone ➔ not able to call the police	police not arrive quickly ➔ not catch the robbers	police not catch the robbers ➔ not get a reward
If I had got up earlier, I wouldn't have missed the bus to school.			

The scene of the crime

● A witness is somebody who sees a crime happen. The police often ask witnesses to give statements. What problems might there be with witness statements?

1 Look at the picture of a crime scene. Read what the witnesses said and note down the inconsistencies in their statements:

Witness A says ... whereas Witness B says ...

Witness A

I was sitting at a café on the opposite side of the square and I saw a man run out of the computer shop carrying something under his right arm. I think it was a laptop computer. He was wearing a blue denim jacket and jeans. He was wearing a baseball cap and the peak covered his eyes so you couldn't really see his face. He bumped into a lady who was carrying some shopping and knocked the shopping out of her hand. He ran towards a black car, near to where I was sitting. There was somebody sitting in the driver's seat of the car and they drove off very quickly towards the motorway.

Witness B

I was just outside the electrical shop, next to the newsagent's, and I saw a man run out and cross the square. He was carrying a laptop under his left arm. He was wearing a black jacket and blue jeans. I didn't see his face because he was running away from where I was standing. But I remember he was wearing a baseball cap back-to-front – with the peak at the back. As he was running across the square, he seemed to bump into someone because she dropped her shopping as he passed and she shouted at him. He ran over to a black van which was parked at the other side of the square. He jumped in it and he drove off.

2 Compare what you've written with what your partner has written and answer these questions.

1 Did you and your partner note down the same things?

2 How many inconsistencies in the witness statements are there?

3 Compare the statements with the picture. Who gives the more accurate statement, Witness A or Witness B?

Writing

3 Imagine you were in the square shown in the picture in Exercise 1 and you witnessed the scene. Write a statement for the police describing what you saw. Give as many details as possible. Use the statements in Exercise 1 as a model.

4 How good a witness would you be? Think back to the start of the lesson you are now in. Describe what happened in the first minute of the lesson, starting from the time the classroom door was closed. Give as many details as possible.

5 Work in small groups. Compare the statements you wrote for Exercise 4.

1 Add to or correct your statements in the light of your discussion.

2 What does this exercise tell you about how people experience the same event?

Project: Write a statement

6 Imagine you witnessed one of the crimes described in these headlines.

Shoplifter gets away with a trolley full of groceries in broad daylight

Mugger on a bike caught after stealing boy's mobile phone

Attempted arson attack prevented by quick-thinking schoolgirl

1 Write a statement saying what you saw. Remember the following:

- Tell the story in chronological order. In other words, describe the events in the order in which they occurred.
- Only give facts, not opinions.
- If you're not sure of something, don't say it.
- If you heard anybody say anything, quote their exact words.

2 When you have written your first draft, ask another student to read it and comment on it.

3 Write your final draft.

4 Put the witness statements for each headline together in a classroom display.

A performance in English

- **Topics** Theatre traditions; people who work in the theatre; scriptwriting
- **Use of English** *Used to* and *would* for repeated actions and events in the past; prepositions following nouns and adjectives

All the world's a stage

- Compare the experience of seeing a play at the theatre and seeing a film at the cinema.

Reading

1 Read about three theatre traditions. Which of them still exists today?

In Ancient Greece plays were performed at the Festival of Dionysus in March and April. This was when the sailing season started. People used to come to Athens from all over the Greek world to see the plays.

The Greeks loved competition. The playwrights would compete against one another to write the best play. They were each sponsored by a rich man who would pay for the production. Each member of a specially selected jury voted for the play which they thought was the best. The play with the most votes won. If you were the winner, your name and your sponsor's name were written on the walls of the theatre for everyone to see. No prize money was involved; it was all about glory.

The plays were performed in open-air theatres. The audience sat in tiered rows in a semi-circle or horse-shoe shape. In both comedies and tragedies, only three actors performed all the speaking roles. The actors wore masks, which made it possible to change character. In addition to the actors, there was a chorus of 12 people who would comment on the action as it was happening. The three best-known playwrights, Aeschylus, Sophocles and Euripides, wrote tragedies. They were all Athenians and all lived in the 5th century BCE.

Kabuki, the popular theatre of Japan, has captured the hearts and minds of audiences from its appearance at the beginning of the seventeenth century to the present day. Plays range from realistic tragic dramas to fantastic adventure stories. Music and dance are skilfully employed, bringing to life characters from the Japanese past, both real and imaginary. Impressive costumes and make-up, and startling stage effects, add to the drama.

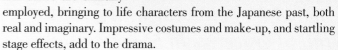

The 'Theatre of Shadows' is an ancient art form, still performed today in **Java, Indonesia** and neighbouring islands. Modern performances can last through the night and are carried out by a single puppeteer who manipulates the characters, often two in one hand. The puppeteer speaks the parts of all the characters and conducts the accompanying music performed by a *gamelan* orchestra, beating the time with a wooden hammer held in his toes.

*This puppet depicts Bima, one of the heroes of the Indian epic, the **Mahabharata**. It was used in performances of this epic during a 'Theatre of Shadows' performance at the Javanese court.*

The Odeon of Herodes Atticus in Athens

2 Read the text again. Then answer the questions.

Ancient Greece

1 Why were plays performed in Athens in March and April?

2 What was the purpose of the competition?

3 What was the advantage of wearing masks?

4 Would there be any disadvantages in having only three actors? What would they be?

5 Are there any competitions today that have similarities with the drama competitions of Ancient Greece?

Kabuki

6 For how long has Kabuki been popular?

7 Are Kabuki plays a reliable way of finding out about Japanese history? Give reasons for your answer.

8 What do you think makes Kabuki a popular art form?

'Theatre of Shadows'

9 What is the main difference between the 'Theatre of Shadows' and the other two types of theatre described on these pages?

10 What skills would you need to be a shadow puppeteer?

Vocabulary

3 Work in pairs. Check the meaning of the words and phrases you don't know.

A: What is a 'playwright'?

B: It's a person who writes plays.

A: It's a funny spelling! I wonder why it's 'wright', not 'write'.

B: What does 'tiered' mean?

A: I don't know. Let's look it up.

Use of English: *Used to* and *would*

You can use *used to* and *would* to refer to past habits.

People used to come to Athens from all over the Greek world to see the plays.

The playwrights would compete against one another to write the best play.

But notice that only used to can be used for past states, e.g. with verbs *be, have, live.*

That old building used to be a theatre. NOT *That old building would be a theatre.*

4 Complete the text using *used to* or *would* with the appropriate verb from the list. Use each verb once. Note: both *used to* and *would* are possible in all cases except one.

| come | forget | live | write | play | play |

When I was a child, we _____¹ in an old house which had quite a big terrace. I always wanted to be an actor and the terrace was my open-air theatre! I _____² plays and I _____³ all the parts myself. My mum and my grandmother _____⁴ up to the terrace to watch them. Sometimes my grandfather _____⁵ the guitar at my performances. Then, when I had two younger brothers and a sister, I became the playwright, director and leading actor. My brothers _____⁶ their lines so I had to be the prompter as well.

Writing and speaking

5 Work in pairs. Write down five things you used to enjoy doing when you were a child. Then tell your partner about them.

I used to play with my toy cars all the time. I would pretend I was the manager of a garage and my friends were the customers.

On stage, off stage

- What do you know about the people who work in a theatre?

Vocabulary

1 Choose two descriptions from the list to match each job. (You will find out whether your answers are correct in the next exercise.)

1 The director

2 The actors

3 The stage manager

4 The set designer

5 The costume designer

6 The lighting and sound technicians

7 The backstage crew

a has the responsibility of making sure the actors are on the stage at the right time.

b is responsible for finding the costumes that the actors are to wear.

c decides how the play is going to be performed.

d bring characters to life on stage using speech, movement and expressions.

e has to be very knowledgeable about fashion and clothes.

f needs to be good with people because he / she has to get the actors to do what he / she wants.

g is responsible for what the stage will look like for each scene.

h gives instructions to the scene painters and the scenery makers.

i have to be capable of moving heavy scenery quickly and efficiently.

j is responsible for everything during a performance including props and scene changes (it's not a job for anyone who's afraid of hard work!).

k have to be good at interpreting the technical effects that the director wants.

l must have a good memory.

m need to be good with their hands because they sometimes have to make scenery.

n are capable of creating effects (including special effects) that add to what the actors are doing on stage.

Listening (31)

2 Listen and check your answers to Exercise 1.

3 Listen again and answer the questions.

1 Where does the talk take place?

2 Who is talking and what is the purpose of her talk?

3 What can you say about her abilities and personality?

4 What do we find out about the play that is on at the theatre at the moment?

5 Do you think the person giving the talk would be a good person to work for? Give your reasons.

Use of English: Prepositions following nouns and adjectives

It's important to know which prepositions follow certain nouns and adjectives.

Here are some examples:
He has the responsibility of making sure the actors are on the stage at the right time.
She is responsible for finding the costumes that the actors are to wear.
She has to be very knowledgeable about fashion and clothes.
They are capable of creating effects, including special effects.
It's not a job for anyone who's afraid of hard work!
They have to be good at interpreting the technical effects that the director wants.
They need to be good with their hands because they sometimes have to make scenery.

Writing

4 **Rewrite these sentences, using the prompts.**

1 She is an expert on theatre traditions in Japan.
(*knowledgeable*)
She is very knowledgeable about theatre traditions in Japan.

2 He's a good actor but do you think he could play Spiderman?
(*capable*)

3 Whose job is it to paint the scenery?
(*responsible*)

4 Who has the job of paying the actors?
(*responsibility*)

5 To work in the backstage crew, it's important that you don't have a fear of heights.
(*afraid*)

6 She gets on very well with people.
(*good*)

5 **Write six descriptions of people you know, using each of the prompts in Exercise 4.**

1 My older brother is very knowledgeable about Formula 1 racing. He knows all the teams, the drivers and their cars.

6 **Work in groups. Try to imagine what it must be like to be a professional actor. What are the advantages and disadvantages?**

I think it must be quite exciting because ...
Yes, but on the other hand, ...

From script to performance

Project: Diary of an (Un)teenager – the play

1 Work in pairs. What do you remember about the extract from *Diary of an (Un)teenager* on page 21? Who are Spencer and Zac?

2 You're going to learn how to write a script. Read the extract below. Then look at the dramatised version on the next page. What is the same? What is different?

3 Now write the script for the rest of Scene 2, based on the following extract. Use the script on page 147 as a model.

Diary of an (Un)teenager

Chapter 1

A Terrible Shock

Friday, May 29th

Strange things have started happening. I feel the need to write these important events down in a diary.

Zac rang me this evening, dear diary. He said, "Hi, Spencer! When you see me tonight you may get a shock!"

He wouldn't say any more.

He was upstairs when I went round to his house.

I opened the door to his bedroom and then stepped back in horror.

I'd never expected this.

I blinked. But Zac was still there – and wearing ... a blue shirt that looked huge on him, the baggiest white trousers I'd ever seen and massive trainers with a huge flap and no laces.

"Why on earth are you dressed like that?" I gasped.

Zac swallowed hard, then announced, "Because, Spencer, I'm a skater now.'

"But you haven't even got a skateboard."

"Not yet, I haven't," he agreed. "But I'm getting one next week. And you don't really need a skateboard these days. You've just got to have the right gear."

Then he put on this top with a hood.

"Once you've got your hoodie, you're a skater. It's as simple as that."

He smiled at me. I tried to smile back but I just couldn't.

"So how much did all this gear cost you?" I asked. "And have you still got the receipt?"

Zac whispered the price to me. I nearly passed out with shock. He'd used up all his birthday money on this rubbish. And nearly half of all his savings too.

I just couldn't believe it.

Zac and I had never wasted any of our money on clothes before. We'd been fine wearing the same shirt and jeans for years.

So what had happened to him?

"Just why have you decided to be a skater?" I asked, finding it hard to control my voice.

Zac started pacing around his room. He sighed heavily.

"It's ever since I turned 13. It's made me think about my life." His voice rose. "I've got to be something."

Will I soon start throwing all my money away on stupid clothes?

No, dear diary, I won't.

I am going to stay EXACTLY as I am now.

And that's a promise, signed here in my diary.

Title: ——————— Diary of an (Un)teenager

Scene 1: Spencer's room at home ———————————

Scene: Where does it take place?

Characters: Who is in the scene? ——

Characters: SPENCER, a 12-year-old boy;

ZAC, a 13-year-old boy

Give the stage directions in brackets. Include details of props and costumes.

(SPENCER is sitting in his room, talking on his mobile phone. He's wearing an old T-shirt and jeans. On his desk is a diary which is open and there's a pen on it to show he's been writing in it. ZAC is off stage and he is talking to SPENCER on the phone.)

Write the characters' names in capital letters to show who is speaking.

ZAC: Hi, Spencer! When you see me tonight, you may get a shock!

When a character starts to speak, put a colon (:) after their name.

SPENCER: What do you mean?

ZAC: You'll see.

SPENCER: What?

ZAC: See you later.

(The lights go down with SPENCER looking puzzled.)

Scene 2: Zac's room at home

(ZAC is in his room. He is wearing a huge blue shirt, very baggy white trousers and big trainers with a huge flap and no laces.)

When a character comes on to the stage after the start of the scene, write 'Enter' followed by the name of the character. When they leave, write 'Exit' and the name of the character.

(Enter SPENCER.)

(SPENCER opens the door to ZAC's room and steps back in horror. He blinks in surprise.)

Where necessary, describe how an actor should say the line.

SPENCER: (shocked) Why on earth are you dressed like that?

(ZAC swallows hard before answering.)

ZAC: Because, Spencer, I'm a skater now.

4 In your pairs, rehearse your script. Then take it in turns to perform Scenes 1 and 2 in front of the class. Vote on the best performance. (You can't vote for yourselves!)

5 If you want to do a performance for other students in the school, choose the director, the actors, a stage manager, the set designer, the costume designer, lighting and sound technicians and the backstage crew.

Fiction ③²

The No. 1 Ladies' Detective Agency
Alexander McCall Smith

1 Read the extract on page 149. Mma Ramotswe is a private detective. She is on her way to solve a crime. How does she feel and why?

2 Read the extract again and answer the questions.

1 How does Mma Ramotswe know where she's going?
2 What time of day is it?
3 What is the road like?
4 What does Mma Ramotswe notice about the condition of the house?
5 Why doesn't Mma Ramotswe go straight to the door when she arrives?

3 Answer these questions about the style of the extract.

1 Look at the first paragraph. There is no main verb. What is the effect of this?
2 Look at the second paragraph. One phrase is repeated. What is it? What is Mma Ramotswe's impression of this place?
3 If you were making a film of this book, what would the film show for the first three paragraphs?
4 In paragraph four, which words and phrases express Mma Ramotswe's feeling of discomfort?
5 Why does the writer use the passive in the phrase 'she felt that she was being watched'?
6 Why does the writer introduce the setotojane beetle?

4 Work in small groups. Discuss this question: how does the writer build tension in this extract?

5 Imagine that Mma Ramotswe wrote a diary entry describing her visit to the house. What would she have written? Write the diary entry in 150 words or fewer.

I set out in the morning with the map that Mr Gotso ...

THE NO. 1 LADIES' DETECTIVE AGENCY

A dusty track hardly in use, enough to break the springs; a
hill, a tumble of boulders, just as the sketch map drawn by
Mr Charlie Gotso had predicted; and above, stretching from
horizon to horizon, the empty sky, singing in the heat of the
5 noon.

Mma Ramotswe steered the tiny white van cautiously,
avoiding the rocks that could tear the sump from the car,
wondering why nobody came this way. This was dead
country; no cattle, no goats; only the bush and the stunted
10 thorn trees. That anybody should want to live here, away from
a village, away from human contact, seemed inexplicable.
Dead country.

Suddenly she saw the house, tucked away behind the
trees almost in the shadow of the hill. It was a bare earth
15 house in the traditional style; brown mud walls, a few
glassless windows, with a knee-height wall around the yard.
A previous owner, a long time ago, had painted designs on
the wall, but their neglect and the years had scaled them off
and only their ghosts remained.

20 She opened the door and eased herself out of the van. The
sun was riding high and its light prickled at her skin. They
were too far west here, too close to the Kalahari, and her
unease increased. This was not the comforting land she had
grown up with; this was merciless Africa, the waterless land.

25 She made her way towards the house, and as she did so she
felt that she was being watched. There was no movement,
but eyes were upon her, eyes from within the house. At the
wall, in accordance with custom, she stopped and called out,
announcing herself.

30 'I am very hot,' she said. 'I need water.'

There was no reply from within the house, but a rustle to
her left, amongst the bushes. She turned round, almost guilty,
and stared. It was a large black beetle, a setotojane, with its
horny neck, pushing at a minute trophy, some insect that had
35 died of thirst perhaps. Little disasters, little victories; like
ours, she thought; when viewed from above we are no more
than setotojane.

'Mma?'

She turned round sharply. A woman was standing in the
40 doorway, wiping her hands on a cloth.

by Alexander McCall Smith

springs (*line 1*) the springs in a car absorb the shock of movement

tumble (*line 2*) (here) a pile that has fallen in a disordered way

boulders (*line 2*) very large stones

noon (*line 5*) 12 o'clock, midday

Mma (*line 6*) a traditional way to address a woman in Bostwana, pronounced 'Ma'

tiny (*line 6*) very small

tear (*line 7*) pull violently

sump (*line 7*) the lower part of an engine containing oil

stunted (*line 9*) small because growth has been stopped

thorn trees (*line 10*) trees with sharp pointed growths on their branches

inexplicable (*line 11*) not able to be explained

tucked away (*line 13*) hidden

bare (*line 14*) without decoration

neglect (*line 18*) not having been cared for

had scaled them off (*line 18*) had caused them to fall off in pieces, like the scales of a fish

eased (*line 20*) moved slowly and carefully

prickled (*line 21*) made her feel a lot of sharp points like needles (on her skin)

merciless (*line 24*) without kindness

in accordance with (*line 28*) following (a rule, a custom)

beetle (*line 33*) an insect with a hard shell-like back

horny (*line 34*) (here) covered in hard, dry skin

minute (*line 34*) pronounced *my-newt,* very small, even smaller than tiny

sharply (*line 39*) suddenly and quickly

wiping (*line 40*) cleaning or drying (with a cloth)

Review of Units 17–18

Vocabulary

Crime

1 Complete the chart.

Crime	Criminal
1 theft	*thief*
2 burglary	_____
3 robbery	_____
4 mugging	_____
5 shoplifting	_____
6 joyriding	_____

2 Write the name of the crime.

1 Stealing a car and driving it fast and dangerously.

2 Assaulting someone in a public place in order to steal from them.

3 Going into a building to steal things from it.

3 Who are these people? Complete the names of the jobs.

1

> I find the clothes that the actors wear on stage. Often this means that I have to have them made.

_____ designer

2

> I have to decide what each scene in the play will look like and I have to design the scenery.

_____ designer

3

> One of the most difficult parts of my job is when a scene is set at night or in the dark but the audience still has to be able to see what is happening on stage.

_____ technician

4

> We're part of the team which makes the scenery and moves it into place during a performance.

_____ crew

5

> My job is to make sure everything goes well during a performance and that all the actors appear on the stage at the right time.

_____ manager

Use of English

4 Complete the crime reports with the correct prepositions.

Owen Chivers, 25, from Portishead, appeared at Bristol Magistrates' Court yesterday. He was accused _____[1] breaking into a jeweller's shop in the shopping centre and stealing jewellery worth £2000. He was also charged _____[2] stealing a car. He pleaded guilty _____[3] both crimes and was sent _____[4] prison for a year.

At Leeds Crown Court yesterday, Ryan Jackson, 35, and Robert Meanwood, 47, were tried _____[5] robbery. This follows a two-year investigation into the raid on a bank in Harehills. Jackson and Meanwood were convicted _____[6] robbery and each sentenced _____[7] five years in prison.

5 Read these sentences. If both *used to* and *would* are possible, circle them both. If only *used to* is possible, circle *used to*.

1 I've always loved stories. When I was very young my parents *used to / would* read a story to me every night.

2 My uncle *used to / would* be a musician in a gamelan orchestra.

3 When my parents were both at work, I *used to / would* go to my friend's house after school.

4 We *used to / would* live in a flat, but now we live in a house.

5 I *used to / would* go to the same school as my cousin, but my family moved house.

6 When my brother was very young, he *used to / would* sing himself to sleep every night.

6 Class 9B are discussing a school trip. Complete what they say using the words in the box.

afraid	
capable	of
knowledgeable	for
responsibility	about
responsible	

1

> Who has the _____ _____ making sure parents knows about the school trip?

2 The school secretary is _____ _____ collecting the money for the trip.

3 We need team leaders who are _____ _____ keeping calm in a crisis and dealing with an emergency.

4 This trip is not suitable for anyone who is _____ _____ heights.

5 Team leaders need to be _____ _____ wildlife and other aspects of the area.

7 Complete the theatre review. Match the two parts of the sentences, putting the verbs into the correct form.

A night to remember? Or a night to forget?

Last night I witnessed one of the worst performances I can ever remember. What went wrong? Well, here's a list.

1 If the actors had had more time to rehearse, they wouldn't have forgotten their lines.

1 If the actors (have) more time to rehearse,

2 If the leading lady's dress (not / be) so long,

3 If the backstage crew (fix) the castle wall correctly,

4 If the sound technician (switch off) the microphones during the interval,

5 If the candle (not / be) so close to the curtain,

6 If the play (not / go) so badly wrong,

 a the curtain (not / catch) fire.

 b they (not / forget) their lines.

 c the audience (not / hear) the stage manager shouting at everyone.

 d it (not / fall down).

 e she (not / fall off) the stage.

 f the audience (stay) for the second act

General knowledge quiz

8 Work in pairs. Ask and answer the questions.

1 Which of these countries has the lowest age of criminal responsibility: Sweden, Switzerland or Japan?

2 There are four countries in the United Kingdom: England, Wales, Northern Ireland and one other. What is it?

3 What do you call the crime of setting fire to something, especially a building, in order to damage or destroy it?

4 In which months was the Festival of Dionysus celebrated in Ancient Greece?

5 Who were Aeschylus, Sophocles and Euripides and what did they have in common?

6 What is Kabuki and when did it first appear?

7 What type of music would accompany a performance of the 'Theatre of Shadows' in Java?

8 What do you call the instructions to actors that appear in a play script?

9 Which two words appear in a play script to show when an actor comes on to and leaves the stage?

10 What do you call the small objects, such as books, candles, umbrellas and so on, that are used by actors during a play?

Acknowledgements

The authors and publishers acknowledge the following sources of copyright material and are grateful for the permissions granted. While every effort has been made, it has not always been possible to identify the sources of all the material used, or to trace all copyright holders. If any omissions are brought to our notice, we will be happy to include the appropriate acknowledgements on reprinting.

p.10 adapted from "People you might know: Identical twin sisters, 26, separated at birth and brought up 4,000 miles apart describe the moment they discovered each other on Facebook" by Mia de Graaf, *The Daily Mail Online*, 13/11/2014, copyright © Solo Syndication, 2014; pp.21, 146-147 from *Diary of an (Un)teenager* by Pete Johnson, Barrington Stoke Ltd. 2004 © Pete Johnson. Reproduced with permission; p.28 adapted from "International body language: a language with no words" by Anne Merritt, *The Telegraph*, 14/05/2013, copyright © Telegraph Media Group Limited 2013; p.30 adapted from 'The Paradox of Music-Evoked Sadness: An Online Survey' by Liila Taruffi and Stefan Koelsch, *PLOS One*, 20/10/2014, DOI: 10.1371/journal.pone.0110490; p.37 from the Prologue in *Lang Lang: Playing with Flying Keys* by Lang Lang as told to Michael French, copyright © 2008 by Lang Lang. Reproduced by permission of Delacorte Press, an imprint of Random House Children's Books, a division of Penguin Random House LLC, all rights reserved; p.40 from *Serve to Win* by Novak Djokovic, published by Bantam Press, 2013. Reproduced by permission of The Random House Group Limited and Penguin Random House LLC; p.47 "Which of these devices or types of media do you use daily or several times a week?" http://www.statista.com/statistics/381293/teenagers-leisure-time-media-usage-by-gender-germany. Reproduced with permission of Statista GmbH; p.50 adapted from "Average person now spends more time on their phone and laptop than sleeping, study claims" by Madlen Davies, *The Daily Mail Online*, 11/03/15, copyright © Solo Syndication, 2015; p.52 "Old pond", "Friends part", "Wake butterfly" and "Violets", published in *On Love and Barley: Haiku of Basho* by Matsui Basho, translated by Lucien Stryk, pp.27, 30, 32, 33, 35, Penguin Classics, 1985, copyright © Lucien Stryk, 1985. Reproduced by permission of Penguin Books Ltd; p.53 'Haikus' by John Foster, published in *The Works*, Macmillan Children's Books 2000, p.207. Reproduced by kind permission of John Foster; p.53 'Summer haiku' by Wendy Cope, published in *The Poetry Store*, Hodder Children's Books, 2005, p.95. Reproduced by permission of United Agents (www.unitedagents. co.uk) on behalf of Wendy Cope © Wendy Cope 2005; p.53 'NoHaiku' by Adrian Henri, published in *The Works*, Macmillan Children's Books 2000, p.209, copyright © Adrian Henri. Reproduced by permission of the author c/o Rogers Coleridge & White., 20 Powis Mews, London W11 1JN; p.53 "Lowku Haiku" by Roger Stevens, published in *The Works*, Macmillan Children's Books 2000, p.209. Reproduced by kind permission of Roger Stevens; p.53 'Haiku' by John Cooper Clarke, published in *The Works*, Macmillan Children's Books 2000, p.210. Reproduced by kind permission of John Cooper Clarke; p.69 from "A Yorkshire Childhood" by George Oldfield, published in *Pandaemonium 1660-1886: The Coming of the Machine as Seen by Contemporary Observers* edited by Marie-Louise Jennings, Icon Books Ltd, 2012, pp.214-215. Reproduced with permission; p.85 from *A Little History of the World* by E. H. Gombrich, translated by Caroline Mustill, Yale University Press. Reproduced with permission; p.91 information about Australian Army Cadets adapted from http://www.armycadets.gov.au/activities/, copyright © Commonwealth of Australia; p.94 'Top 25 jobs according to 13- to 14-year-old British teenagers' from "Nothing in Common: The Career Aspirations of Young Britons Mapped Against Projected Labour Market Demand 2010-2020", 19/03/2013 by Dr Anthony Mann, David Massey, Peter Glover, Elnaz T. Kashefpadkel and James Dawkins, copyright © Education & Employers; Statistics on p.108 from http://www.cambridge-water.co.uk/customers/how-much-water-do-you-use, copyright © Cambridge Water; p119 extract from 'They Don't Mean It!' by Lensey Namioka, from *First Crossing: Stories about Teen Immigrants*, Candlewick Press 2004, used with kind permission of Lensey Namioka; pp.126-127 adapted from 'Pepper's Ghost' by Paul Curzon and Peter McOwan, www.cs4fn.org, Queen Mary University of London. Reproduced with permission; p.130 adapted from *English Vocabulary in Use Upper-Intermediate with answers* by Michael McCarthy and Felicity O'Dell, 1994, copyright © Cambridge University Press. Reproduced with permission; p.133 'The Sound Collector" by Roger McGough from *Pillow Talk*, copyright © Roger McGough, 1990. Reproduced by permission of United Agents (www.unitedagents.co.uk) on behalf of Roger McGough; p.133 "SSHH!" by Les Baynton, published in *The Poetry Store*, Hodder Children's Books, 2005, p.258. Reproduced by kind permission of Les Baynton; p.142 about Kabuki and Theatre of Shadows, www.britishmuseum.org © Trustees of the British Museum, 2016; p.149 from *The No. 1 Ladies' Detective Agency* by Alexander McCall Smith, Birlinn Limited, 2004, pp.220-221, reproduced by permission of David Higham Associates.

Thanks to the following for permission to include images:

Cover artwork mtphoto19 / Alamy Stock Photo

pp.8tr, 9tr,11tr,13tr KreativeKolors/Shutterstock; p.8l Creatas/Thinkstock; p.8cl violetblue/Shutterstock; p.8cr iStock/Thinkstock; p.8r szefei/Shutterstock; p.10 Dustin Finkelstein/Getty Images Entertainment; p.11 Anton_Ivanov/Shutterstock; p.13 monsterslippers.co.uk; pp.14tr, 15tr, 17tr, 19tr, 21tr, 23tr muznabutt/Shutterstock; p.14l paul Prescott/Shutterstock; p.14r Uwe Ommer, used with permission; p.16l Hugo Felix/Shutterstock; p.16cl wong sze yuen/Shutterstock; p.16cr Kseniia Perminova/Shutterstock; p.14r Kerry Garvey/Shutterstock; p.18l Popperfoto/Getty Images; p.18b Shutterstock/Mascha Tace; p.19 SSPL/Getty Images; p.20t prudkov/Shutterstock; p.22tl Sedlacek/Shutterstock; p.22bl indira's work/

Shutterstock; p.22tr James Flint/Shutterstock; p.22cr Yeko Photo Studio/Shutterstock; p.22br Fabio Lamanna/Shutterstock; p.23 Lilyana Vynogradova/Shutterstock; pp.24tr, 25tr, 27tr, 29tr, maradon 333/Shutterstock; p.24(1) CREATISTA/Shutterstock; p.24(2,3,7) PathDoc/Shutterstock; p.24(4) Chepko Danil Vitalevich/Shutterstock; p.24(5) Suzanne Tucker/Shutterstock; p.24(6) ProStockStudio/Shutterstock; p.26 DmitriMaruta/Shutterstock; p.28 Asier Romero/Shutterstock; pp.30tr, 31tr, 33tr, 35tr, 37tr, 39tr Petr Vaclavek/Shutterstock; p.30 Dragon Images/Shutterstock; p.32 Frank Hoensch/Getty Images; p.33l Dmitry Skutin/Shutterstock; p.33cl cowardlion/Shutterstock; p.33cr Furtseff/Shutterstock; p.33r Mikhail Bakunovich/Shutterstock; p.34tr Henry Groskinsky/The LIFE Images Collection/Getty Images; p.34br CBW/Alamy Stock Photo; p.35 Maksym Bondarchuk/Shutterstock; p.36 james cheadle/Alamy Stock Photo; p.38 Sentavio/Shutterstock; p.39tl Fotoluminate LLC/Shutterstock; p.39bl ZouZou/Shutterstock; p.39br iStock/Thinkstock; p.40tr, 41tr, 43tr, 45tr kazoka/Shutterstock; p.40 Neale Cousland/Shutterstock; p.42 Glinskaja Olga/Shutterstock; p.45l Portrait of a Lady thought to be Lady Mary Wortley Montagu (1689-1762) (oil on panel), Knapton, George (1698-1778)/Private Collection/Photo © Christie's Images/Bridgeman Images; p.45r Edward Jenner (1749-1823) performing the first vaccination against smallpox in 1796, 1879 (oil on canvas) (detail) (see also 166614), Melingue, Gaston (1840-1914)/Academie Nationale de Medecine, Paris, France/Archives Charmet/Bridgeman Images; pp.46tr, 47tr, 49tr, 51tr, 53tr, 55tr Twin Design/Shutterstock; pp.47br, 88 oliveromg/Shutterstock; p.48 Kues/Shutterstock; p.50 Photographee.eu/ Shutterstock; p.55 Graphicworld/Shutterstock; p.56tr, 57tr, 59tr, 61tr Vaclav Volrab/Shutterstock; p.56 Colin D.Young/Shutterstock; p.59tl OlegD/Shutterstock; p.59bl auremar/Shutterstock; p.59tr Superlime/Shutterstock; pp.60–61 Sergey Nivens/ Shutterstock; p.62tr, 63tr, 65tr, 67tr, 69tr, 71tr Print Collector/Getty Images; p.62c Christian Vinces/Shutterstock; p.62r Jaochainoi/Shutterstock; p.64 Mary Evans Picture Library; p.65 SSPL/Getty Images; pp.66t, 71b Bryan Donkin Archive Trust/Science Museum/ Science & Society Picture Library; p.66b Tudgay, Frederick, 1841-1921, *The "Dunedin" off the English Coast*, 1875, 02/01, Hocken Collections, Uare Taoka o Hākena, University of Otago; p.68 Hulton Archive/Stringer/Getty Images; p.69 Time Life Pictures/Mansell/The LIFE Picture Collection/Getty Images; p.71t The Art Archive/Alamy Stock Photo; p.72tr, 73tr, 75tr, 77tr Oleksiy Mark/Shutterstock; p.72 muzsy/Shutterstock; p.74, 80tl Monkey Business Images/Shutterstock; p.76 koya979/Shutterstock; p.77 S_L/Shutterstock; pp.78tr, 79tr, 81tr, 83tr, 85tr, 87tr Neil Webb/Getty Images; p.79 gorillaimages/Shutterstock; p.80bl Olga Danylenko/Shutterstock; p.80tr LI CHAOSHU/Shutterstock; p.82tr Rido/Shutterstock; p.82bl Magcom/Shutterstock; pp.82bl, 87 Eric Isselee/Shutterstock; pp.82bc, 87 Serdar Tibet/ Shutterstock; pp.82bc, 87 GTS Productions/Shutterstock; pp.82br, 87 Chris Howey/ Shutterstock; p.85l wongstock/Shutterstock; p.85c DutchScenery/Shutterstock; p.85r Dudarev Mikhail/Shutterstock; p.86tl Filip Dokladal/Shutterstock; p.86cl Everett Historical/ Shutterstock; p.86bl Robert Adrian Hillman/Shutterstock; p.86tr wawritto/Shutterstock; p.88tr, 89tr, 91tr, 93tr Fanatic Studio/Shutterstock; p.91t Azuresong84/Shutterstock; p.91b Department of Defence/ADF; p.93l Ulrich Doering/Alamy Stock Photo; p.93r Volt Collection/ Shutterstock; pp.94tr, 95tr, 97tr, 99tr, 101tr, 103tr donfiore/Shutterstock; p.94 auremar/ Shutterstock; pp.96l, 96c, 96r, 97, 109l, 124, 126tr, 127tr, 129tr, 131tr, 133tr, 135tr iStock/Getty Images; p.98tl wizdata/Shutterstock; p.98tc Strejman/Shutterstock; p. 98tr stockyimages/Shutterstock; p.98bl photo and logo used with kind permission of TeenTech; p.98cr Conor Lynch Woodturning; p.100 Mary Evans Picture Library/Alamy Stock Photo; p.101 from Project Gutenburg; p.103tr Francesco Abrignani/Shutterstock; p.103cr Morphart Creation/Shutterstock; p.103br Mr Aesthetics/Shutterstock; p.104tr, 015tr, 107tr, 109tr Andrea Danti/Shutterstock; p.106 YOSHIKAZU TSUNO/Getty Images; p.109c diak/ Shutterstock; p.109r shao weiwei/Shutterstock; pp.110tr, 111tr, 113tr, 115tr, 117tr, 119tr AnVino/Shutterstock; p.111t MJTH/Shutterstock; p.111b Olena Zaskochenko/Shutterstock; p.112t The Asahi Shimbun/Getty Images; p.112b Arif Ali/AFP/Getty Images; p.119 Delmas Lehman/Shutterstock; p.120tr, 121tr, 123tr, 125tr kentoh/Shutterstock; p.120l Roxana Bashyrova/Shutterstock; p.120tl Nataliya Hora/Shutterstock; p.120c ILYA AKINSHIN/ Shutterstock; p.120r Cristi Lucaci/Shutterstock; p.121 Pressmaster/Shutterstock; p.122t SHENG LI/Reuters/Corbis; p.122b © THE UNSEEN 2016 Photograph by Jonny Lee; p.125 radoma/Shutterstock; p.126 Mary Evans Picture Library; p.127 Vivien Kililea/Getty Images for Flaunt Magazine; p.128tr © Cecilia Bleasdale, used by kind permission; p.128bl artivo/Shutterstock; p.128cr kuleczka/Shutterstock; p.128br monbibi/Shutterstock; p.128br inxti/Shutterstock; p.128br rzstudio/Shutterstock; p.129l Edward H. Adelson; p.129r with kind permission of Beau Lotto, © lottolab.org; p.130 sumikophoto/Shutterstock; p.131 amenic181/Shutterstock; p.132tr Francesco Abrignani/Shutterstock; p.132cr Wiktoria Pawlak/Shutterstock; p.132br jps/Shutterstock; p.135 De Agostini Picture Library/Getty Images; pp.136tr, 137tr, 139tr, 141tr Rob Wilson/Shutterstock; pp.142tr, 143tr, 145tr, 147tr, 149tr, 151tr LaFifa/ Shutterstock; p.142bl Anastasios71/Shutterstock; p.142cr Koichi Kamoshida/Staff/Getty Images; p.142br snowhite/Shutterstock; p.144–145 Pavel L Photo and Video/Shutterstock; p.148–149 AlexTanya/Shutterstock; p.151r Lana Smirnova/Shutterstock

Illustrations © Cambridge University Press: pp.12, 47, 61, 72, 73, 86, 87, 104, 105, 107, 108, 110, 118, 136, 138, Sharpe Images; pp.27, 92, 133l, 151l David Banks; pp.29, 46, 54, 58, 108, 114, 133r, Phill Burrows; p.52 Fausto Bianchi/Beehive Illustration; p.103l Dusan Pavlic/Beehive Illustration; pp.116, 137, 140 Mark Turner/Beehive Illustration; p.139 Dusan/Pavlic/Beehive Illustration

Image positions: *l* = left, *r* = right, *t* = top, *b* = bottom, *c* = centre